A SENSE OF GOD

Meditations for Thinking Christians

Peter W. Stine

BAKER BOOK HOUSE
Grand Rapids, Michigan 49506

PHOTOLITHOPRINTED BY CUSHING - MALLOY, INC.
ANN ARBOR, MICHIGAN, UNITED STATES OF AMERICA

In loving memory of my parents
Earle and Ione Stine
whose "sense of God"
was obvious to all who knew them

Introduction

About a year after I started teaching English in college, the idea came to me of writing a series of meditations on the compatibility of literature and faith. The first form such thoughts took was oral devotions before my classes. Many students expressed appreciation for these, and it occurred to me that it might be helpful to put some of the better ones into print.

Although I did not then pursue the possibility of publication, I did think of a title for such a collection. In reading William Wordsworth's thoughtful ode, "Intimations of Immortality from Recollections of Early Childhood," I was struck with the final two lines:

> To me the meanest flower that blows can give
> Thoughts that do often lie too deep for tears.

"Too deep for tears"; what a striking image! The poet was confirming what I had long suspected: that we are capable of thoughts so profound and feelings so strong that they lie below the ordinary modes of expression. They reside in that spiritual side of our nature which is a direct reflection of the *imago Dei*, the image of God, and to which literature is so accessible an entrance. "Too Deep for Tears"—an ideal title for reflections on the relationship between the art of literary expression and spiritual faith.

For all the enthusiasm I felt about such a project, it was to lie dormant for a dozen years. But then a member of the editorial staff of The Salvation Army's weekly news and inspirational magazine, *The War Cry*, asked me if I would consider writing a column on faith and literature. To his obvious surprise, I immediately answered that not only would I be happy to undertake such a project, but that I knew what I wanted to call it. The column, "Too Deep for Tears," is still appearing weekly in *The War Cry*; it is by the kindness of The Salvation Army and its editorial staff that the material from past issues of *The War Cry* is reprinted here.

And so to the present volume. It is my profound hope that many of you who read these pieces will find them helpful, and even stimulating. The title, "A Sense of God," though not of my choosing, is a good one, for there is in every piece of created art—whether in syllables, in oils, or in chords—a sense of that One who is the Source of all creation. And the phrase, "Meditations for Thinking Christians" notes that as children of God we are expected to be thinking—as well as thoughtful—citizens of that kingdom whose emissaries we have been called to be.

May God often give you feelings, ideas, and thoughts that "lie too deep for tears."

Peter W. Stine
February, 1980

1

Emily Dickinson spoke of books as "frigates" on which we can sail far away and discover new lands, ideas, and experiences we never thought possible. We can visit Victorian England with that most amiable of guides, Charles Dickens; explore the wilderness of the north with Jack London; glide through the shadowy back streets of New England towns with Nathaniel Hawthorne; go whaling with Herman Melville, warring with Leo Tolstoy, or fishing with Ernest Hemingway—the list is endless.

When God created us, He gave us the powers to understand, to create, to imagine, to dream. But many of us have so ignored these powers that they have become stunted. God wants us to be *whole* people, so that we can serve Him with all our hearts, minds, and strength. If you are not a reader—if the very idea of picking up a novel or collection of short stories is foreign to you—you are allowing a vital part of you to grow weak. This was not God's intent when He looked at His creation and saw that it was good.

2

One of the masterpieces of world literature is "The Inferno," by Dante Alighieri (1265–1321). It is a description of a journey through hell, and is part of his larger work, *The Divine Comedy*. In Dante's hell, the sinners are given "symbolic retribution"; that is, they are punished in ways related to the sins they committed on earth. For example, those guilty of graft are sunk in boiling pitch (symbolic of their sticky fingers); thieves are perpetually covered with reptiles (reflective of their deceitful ways); fortune-tellers walk through eternity with their heads turned backwards—they cannot see in front of them nor perceive what is to come.

Among the most memorable of the punishments in "The Inferno" is meted out to the hypocrites—those who claimed to be holy and to serve God but were actually ruthless and self-serving. These suffering souls walk in a never-ending circle, weighed down by great leaden robes. The robes are gilded on the outside and shaped like monk's habits, but are actually burdens reminiscent of the deceit practiced during their earthly stay. In John Ciardi's translation, Dante describes this sight:

> About us now in the depth of the pit we found
> a painted people, weary and defeated.
> Slowly, in pain, they paced it round and round.
> All wore great cloaks cut to as ample a size
> as those worn by the Benedictines of Cluny.
> The enormous hoods were drawn over their eyes.

The outside is all dazzle, golden and fair;
　　the inside, lead, so heavy that Frederick's capes,
　　compared to those, would seem as light as air.
O weary mantle for eternity!
　　We turned to the left again along their course,
　　listening to their moans of misery.
But they moved so slowly down that barren strip,
　　tired by their burden, that our company
　　was changed at every movement of the hip.

It is not likely that Dante's description of hell is literally true. But it is accurate in its basic concept: those who follow their own way through the world and ignore God's law will be punished, if in no other way than to be shut away from His presence. To the person who foolishly and casually says that he would not mind going to hell, since that is where most of his friends will be, Dante offers a stern warning. Our earthly deeds have a far-reaching effect on the disposition of our spiritual selves at the end of life. If you want to gamble that Dante—and the Scriptures—is wrong, that there is nothing but void after death, you should remember that the stakes are extremely high. And there will be no way to recoup your losses.

One of the most frequent themes treated by poets and playwrights is the shortness of life and the unreliability of the future. In Shakespeare's great Scottish tragedy, *Macbeth*, there is murder, intrigue, and a great deal of analysis of the meaning of life. Macbeth's career rises meteorically from minor nobleman to king, through the help of his ambitious wife. But by the end of the play, when Macbeth is surrounded by a vast army of rebels, he is devastated by a confrontation with mortality. Word comes that his lady, on whom he has relied so heavily and who was the catalyst for his treacherous actions, is now dead. Macbeth's reaction to this news is desperately philosophic, hopelessly resigned, empty of hope:

> Tomorrow, and tomorrow, and tomorrow,
> Creeps in this petty pace from day to day
> To the last syllable of recorded time;
> And all our yesterdays have lighted fools
> The way to dusty death. Out, out brief candle!
> Life's but a walking shadow, a poor player
> That struts and frets his hour upon the stage
> And then is heard no more: it is a tale
> Told by an idiot, full of sound and fury,
> Signifying nothing.

Some of Macbeth's observations can be confirmed by Scripture. Certainly he is right in affirming the brevity of life; the Bible speaks of life as a vapor and as grass (James 4:14; Ps. 103:15). However, God did not plan for us to be mere "players"—and poor ones at that—strutting and fretting upon the stage of life. Macbeth is also misguided when he thinks that life ends at death, that it is, in fact, "heard no more." Above all, Macbeth is, thank God, completely wrong when he says that life is a disjointed "tale told by an idiot" which, after all is over, "signifies nothing." Christ said that He came not only to give us life but to give us life more abundant (John 10:10). This is the victory which the child of God knows will last far beyond "the last syllable of recorded time." But the non-Christian, who speaks only the language of what the apostle Paul calls "the flesh," cannot understand the concept of eternal life (see Rom. 8:5). By his own refusal to accept God's gift, the unbeliever is relegated to that dark and hopeless world described so eloquently and futilely by Macbeth.

The quality of mercy is not strained,
It droppeth as the gentle rain from heaven
Upon the place beneath; it is twice blessed:
It blesseth him that gives and him that takes ...
It is an attribute to God himself;
And earthly power doth then show likest God's
When mercy seasons justice.

Although this eloquent speech from *The Merchant of Venice* was originally made in a courtroom, its meaning goes far beyond the limited context of formal law. Genuine sympathy for a wrongdoer is sometimes difficult to conjure up, especially if the offense has been directed at oneself. In such a case, mercy is often obscured by an emotional wave of fright, anger, and the desire for revenge. This separates "him that gives and him that takes" in mutual contempt rather than joining them in an assurance of forgiveness.

Jesus considered mercy important enough to include it in the honor roll of virtues known as the Beatitudes. His admonition to Peter to forgive "seventy times seven" and His warning against the hasty condemnation of the woman taken in sin are further evidences; His plea on the cross for the forgiveness of His tormentors is perhaps the supreme model in the exercise of mercy.

Portia is correct when she describes mercy as a divine attribute. She is equally accurate when she says that man is closer to what God originally intended when he uses mercy in the conduct of his daily life.

5

William Shakespeare was not only one of the greatest dramatists of all time; he was also a master poet. One of his sonnets has this lovely beginning:

> When to the sessions of sweet silent thought
> I summon up remembrance of things past,
> I sigh the lack of many a thing I sought,
> And with old woes new wail my dear time's waste.

We all tend to look to the past, savoring the sweet times of accomplishment and lamenting the frustrating periods of failure. Along with such reminiscences we also evaluate the way our time has been spent and the kinds of goals we have pursued.

This process can be either productive or disappointing. If we can learn from our errors in judgment and from our pursuits of things which were only partially or temporarily satisfying, we are the better for our ransacking of the attic of our past. There is little value, however, of longing looks over the shoulder if we lose sight of the view in front of us.

The Christian is not exempt from memories of experiences which have been fruitless or ill-advised. However, he has the glorious option of following Paul's advice to forget the past and concentrate on the present which will, in turn, make the future all the more secure (Phil. 3:13, 14).

A man is poor indeed whose only inheritance from yesterday is a legacy of regret. A Christian need not be concerned with "things past," but can claim his birthright in the kingdom of God with eternally bright prospects.

6

Read these words of Shakespeare aloud:

> Sweet are the uses of adversity,
> Which, like the toad, ugly and venomous,
> Wears yet a precious jewel in his head.

Rare is the human being who can recognize the advantages of misfortune or reap a profit from his own unhappiness. Our fallen state limits our vision, so we often see only the immediate chaos, rather than the more positive, far-reaching implications of our plight. Such short-sightedness is, alas, the curse of the human race; and it usually brings despair at a time when hope is badly needed.

This myopic preoccupation with one's woes is not automatically or even easily resolved for the man who learns truly to love God. However, given enough time, prayer, and faith, such a man can trust Scripture's message: that God is interested in the most minute detail of our lives, and that He intervenes in our comings and our goings.

Armed with this assurance of divine involvement, the Christian can say with Shakespeare that adversity, while it is inevitable, need not be an unmixed curse. The poet's metaphor of the "ugly and venomous" toad is appropriate; when our lives are filled with difficult or burdensome circumstances we sometimes feel we are plagued as the Egyptians were. What a blessed moment it is

15

when, with a fragment of God-given insight, we can discern precious jewels of value gleaming in what we had previously seen only as intimidating obstacles to our happiness.

7

Even though a scriptural understanding of God's providence does not include the concept of "luck" (good or bad), a case certainly can be made for the occasional arrival of an unusually good *opportunity* which ought not to be ignored. Yet some people lack courage to take advantage of such opportunities when they come, since often the end result is unpredictable—it is not a "sure thing." Others feel uncomfortable with anything other than the normal routine. A chance to travel to an exotic place or to expand knowledge of a little-known subject is seen as a threat rather than a means of growth.

Into the mouth of Brutus, the glorious villain of *Julius Caesar*, Shakespeare has put some words which address this matter of opportunity and growth:

> There is a tide in the affairs of men,
> Which, taken at the flood, leads on to fortune;
> Omitted, all the voyage of their life
> Is bound in shallows and in miseries;
> And we must take the current when it serves,
> Or lose our ventures.

In Shakespeare's play this philosophy becomes the rationale for severe political action. But if we transfer it to the normal course of daily life, we find that a startling contrast is set up by the poet. The choice lies between "fortune" and "shallows and miseries"; between growth and stagnation; between expansion and contraction.

There are a great number of people, both in and out of the company of believers, who are unhappy with their work, their family life, or perhaps with life in general. These same people can often look back to a time when the tide of opportunity swelled for a moment, seeming to pause and allow them a chance to launch. But they lingered too long in indecision, and are now wallowing in murky backwaters. It is not God's plan that any of His creation be discontented or unfulfilled, but neither is He likely to force us to act. It is enough that He sends us the opportunities to grow; it is to ourselves that we must look if we "lose our ventures."

8

One of Shakespeare's early history plays, *Richard III*, opens with these famous words: "Now is the winter of our discontent made glorious summer. . . ." Granted, the reference here is to political change, but what a wonderful description of the transformation possible when the human life is yielded to the will of God.

Many people live in a perpetual state of winter, with all the discomfort and ugliness that state suggests. But others throughout history have discovered that a "glorious summer" is indeed possible, and this has made a great difference in their lives. Famous Christians from Paul to Augustine to Luther to Wesley to C. S. Lewis have recorded their life-changing encounters with Christ. A more recent example is Charles Colson, the former Washington tough man turned prison reformer and contented Christian. While there are some who cynically suggest that he is out for self-gain, the majority of those who read Colson's book or hear him speak are convinced that he has experienced in a spiritual way that wonderful transformation of which Shakespeare's Richard spoke.

Further into the Shakespearean text we are told what happens when this sort of change comes over a country. With war over, "bruised arms are hung up for monuments . . . stern alarms are changed to merry greetings," and, best of all, "grim-visag'd war hath smoothed his wrinkl'd front." These are the fruits of real change, and

19

they can occur in the human life, the family, the community, and the country.

We all know people—perhaps there are some in your own family—who have experienced the "winter of discontent" long enough, and who need to hang up their "bruised arms." Praise God—this is possible, for a change of spiritual climate is ours for the asking. God can make us triumphant in a way old crook-backed Richard never dreamed.

9

The opening years of the seventeenth century in England were rich in literary output. In that period the mature Shakespeare wrote his great tragedies; other playwrights such as Ben Jonson produced plays for the varied dramatic tastes of Jacobite Englishmen; and a new generation of gifted poets emerged. Some of these poets wrote in a thoroughly secular vein, and were sometimes called "Cavalier" poets, while others concerned themselves with subjects (both sacred and worldly) which required a philosophical—even "metaphysical"—treatment. The informal leader of this latter group was John Donne. But also writing in this mode was a man of great spiritual conviction, one of the English language's greatest devotional poets: George Herbert (1593–1633, tutor at Cambridge and parish minister at Bremerton St. Andrew, near Salisbury).

Herbert seems to have had no interest in secular matters, for the concerns of his poetry are entirely spiritual. His major theme was the domination of the spirit by its Creator-God and the reluctance of most men to allow this dominance. Herbert never expected that his poems would be published, and he surely had no idea that 350 years after his death his poems would still be read. It is impossible, however, to bury the kind of fervent devotion and consecration expressed by George Herbert.

His major poetry was crowded into a volume called *The Temple,* which contains such sections as "The Church Porch," "The Church," and "The Church Militant." These include poems about parts of the church, such as the altar, the windows, the monuments, the floor, and the lock and key. In addition there is a rich selection of verses on Bible stories, on parts of the liturgy, and on Herbert's primary theme, the relation of God and man and the struggle for control. Best-known of these is "The Collar," which begins with the speaker's assertion of independence:

> I struck the board, and cried, "No more;
> I will abroad!"
> What? shall I ever sigh and pine?
> My lines and life are free; free as the road,
> Loose as the wind, as large as store.

But the speaker found, as did Jonah and David and thousands since, that he was a captive of his own freedom. In spite of his dissatisfaction with his "rope of sands," in the end he was wise enough to recognize that God's control (the collar of the poem's title) was his only key to liberty:

> But as I rav'd and grew more fierce and wild
> At every word,
> Methought I heard one calling, "Child!"
> And I replied, "My Lord."

For poets in the early seventeenth century (known as "metaphysical" poets), the use of puns, conundrums, shapes, and other devices was considered part of the poet's art. George Herbert, though completely devoted in his subject matter to the glorification of God, used his share of gimmicks to express his praise. As in everything, however, Herbert uses the poetic conventions of the day to praise God.

Perhaps the most elaborate of the unusual techniques of Herbert's time was the "shaped" poem. Herbert created at least two celebrated poems using this device:

The Altar

A broken altar, Lord, Thy servant rears,
Made of a heart, and cemented with tears:
    Whose parts are as Thy hand did frame;
    No workman's tool hath touched the same.
           A   heart   alone
           is   such   a   stone
           As   nothing   but
           Thy power doth cut.
           Wherefore each part
           Of my hard heart
           Meets in this frame
           To praise Thy name:
    That, if I chance to hold my peace,
    These stones to praise Thee may not cease,
O let Thy blessed sacrifice be mine,
And sanctify this altar to be Thine.

Easter Wings

Lord, Who createdst man in wealth and store,
Though foolishly he lost the same
Decaying more and more,
Till he became
Most poor:
With Thee
O let me rise
As larks, harmoniously,
And sing this day Thy victories:
Then shall the fall further the flight in me.

My tender age in sorrow did begin;
And still with sicknesses and shame
Thou didst so punish sin,
That I became
Most thin.
With Thee
Let me combine
And feel this day Thy victory;
For, if I imp my wing on Thine,
Affliction shall advance the flight in me.

Lest the modern reader consider this technique
an idle exercise, note the precise placement of
words in these poems, and observe how theme
and form are perfectly welded. This synthesis reflects the harmony which George Herbert, that
most saintly of sacred poets, felt in the reaches of
his soul.

24

11

Paradox is one of the most convenient tools at the poet's disposal. With it he can change direction at will, add subtlety, and speak on many levels at once. The poets of seventeenth-century England were especially skilled at the use of paradox. An excellent example is John Donne's fourteenth Holy Sonnet, called "Batter My Heart, Three-Personed God." In typical seventeenth-century confessional, autobiographical style, Donne speaks of his struggles with God. The poem, describing his desire to overcome the temptations of the world and the flesh in order to give himself entirely to spiritual matters, is filled with violent images and allusions. The first obvious paradox comes in lines three and four:

That I may rise and stand, o'erthrow me; and bend
Your force to break, blow, burn, and make me new.

You can see the rhetorical powers of contradiction at work: the speaker in the poem claims that unless he is overthrown, he can never "rise and stand." This violent conception of God is more than a mere poetic device; it is the product of Donne's long spiritual struggle.

After six lines in which the speaker casts himself as a "usurped town," waiting for the right king to conquer him, we come to the end of the sonnet and a very startling paradox. Again the theme is the poet's yielding himself to the divine power and the necessity for total surrender before any autonomy can be achieved:

> Take me to You, imprison me, for I,
> Except you enthrall me, never shall be free,
> Nor ever chaste, except You ravish me.

Here we see the remarkable power of poetry to express truths in paradoxical terms. The speaker recognizes that he needs to become God's captive and slave before he can become a free man.

In the rather startling final line, the poet uses sexual language to leave one last strong paradox with the reader: We can never be pure, clean, and "chaste" unless we relinquish and yield ourselves to God's ravishment.

This is a different perspective on the blessed Trinity of Christian lore: the Almighty is presented as a three-personed God who "knocks," "o'erthrows," "imprisons," "enthralls," and "ravishes." Donne's sonnet manifests the great malleability of poetry; it can appear in a variety of forms, using a panoply of tools and devices. Yet it consistently speaks to ideas of significance to every man and woman, even to those for whom poetry is an unknown joy.

12

My mind to me a Kingdom is;
Such present joys therein I find
That it excels all other bliss
That earth affords or grows by kind.
— *Edward Dyer*

Unhappily, some Christians feel that the child of God ought to live by faith alone, and ignore the cultivation of his intellect. True, faith is crucial; we grow by the discipline required in the abdication of our will to God's, and by the lessons of patience learned before His will is made known. But we are also required to be worthy stewards, and to prepare ourselves for the rigors of living in a competitive and challenging society. We do ourselves and God's kingdom a great disservice if we deny the necessity for improving our minds and if we neglect the study of the world.

The speaker in Dyer's poem seems to have reached his eloquent conclusion after considerable searching. He has learned, at long last, that contentment is found by diligently marshalling the resources his Maker has put at his disposal, and by sharing with others the joy of his blessed discovery.

As you read these few lines of poetry out loud to yourself (yes, poetry *always* should be read out loud), think of the implications. Your mind—seat of the memory, repository of sense images, cradle of fantasies, warehouse of facts—is a kingdom over which you have been given dominion. You have responsibility for its growth, or for its inactivity and atrophy; you have control, for the most part, over what goes in it to stay. You certainly have some say about the company it keeps and the neighborhood it loiters in.

If we violate this part of ourselves with polluted reading or rancid thoughts, we are unworthy leaders of this remarkable kingdom. Our intellect ought to bring, as the poet says, "bliss"; God does not will for us to allow it to stroll in the shadows or, perhaps worse yet, to die the slow and paralyzing death brought on by inactivity.

13

John Milton's *Paradise Lost* is the Sistine Chapel ceiling, the B-Minor Mass of English literature. Its structure follows the great epic poems of Homer and Virgil, which tell heroic tales of military escapades, voyages on perilous seas, battle and escape and adventure. But Milton's poem deals with the most monumental event since God created light: the fall of man. Here we see the great drama from beginning to end, from the rebellion of Lucifer in heaven to the stunningly prideful bite of fruit in the Garden of Eden. Milton details the dynamics of the opposition between Lucifer and God, especially after Lucifer's fall from heaven. In one of the most dramatic passages of the poem, Milton describes Satan's expulsion: "... Him the Almighty Power/ Hurled headlong flaming from th' ethereal sky,/ With hideous ruin and combustion, down/ To bottomless perdition, there to dwell/ In adamantine chains and penal fire,/ Who durst defy th' Omnipotent to arms."

As he writes earlier in Book I, Milton's declared intention in *Paradise Lost* is to "justify the ways of God to men." This might seem like a presumptuous statement, until we understand Milton's view of the function of the poet. He considered the gifted writer an interpreter, a liaison between the eternal and the temporal, between the One and the many. Though he was blind, Milton desired to enlighten man's understanding of his spiritual origins and the never-ending spiritual conflict raging over his soul.

To read *Paradise Lost* is to be caught up in its great music, its majestic swell of language. By the time the poem describes the presence of God Himself, the reader is prepared to understand more clearly the majesty and awe which ought rightly to accompany any glimpse, however brief, of Him who made us.

14

One of the great triumphs of Milton's *Paradise Lost* is the slow but certain degradation, both moral and physical, of Satan. Early in the poem, the magnificent fallen angel finds himself prostrate on the floor of that lower region which God created to house him and his cohorts. Satan is never at a loss for words, and his first speeches are masterpieces of rationalization and deception. In one of these he affirms what would later come to be a popular heresy—that heaven and hell alike are found only within the individual: "The mind is its own place, and in itself/ Can make a Heaven of Hell, a Hell of Heaven."

Satan goes on to assert that only on one's own, even in the lower climes, can one be truly free from God's tyranny. And then Milton has this arch-enemy of God state the ultimate heresy, the root of all evil and rebellion: "Better to reign in Hell, than serve in Heav'n."

Here in one terse slogan is the attitude of all sinners everywhere, whether they express it or not. The Christian life consists of yielding oneself to God so He might do with us as He will; Satan's declaration is a direct contradiction of that willingness to be led, to be controlled. Satan's obsession with power caused his expulsion in the first place, and it has fueled his destruction of men ever since.

In refreshingly direct contrast to Satan's ugly

declaration in *Paradise Lost* is David's affirmation: "I had rather be a doorkeeper in the house of my God, than to dwell in the tents of wickedness" (Ps. 84:10).

15

At the beginning of Book III of *Paradise Lost,* God the Father and Christ the Son are in heaven watching Satan wing his way through the chaos. His destination is the newly created earth, where he will try to destroy man; his motive is revenge against God for casting him out of heaven. Into God's mouth Milton puts these ominous words: "For man will hearken to his glozing lies,/ And easily transgress the sole command,/ Sole pledge of his obedience; so will fall/ He and his faithless progeny. Whose fault?/ Whose but his own? Ingrate, he had of me/ All he could have; I made him just and right,/ Sufficient to have stood, though free to fall."

Milton's startling point is that God puts the burden for the fall, for sin, and for death (they all go together) squarely on man's shoulders. God knows that man will succumb to the subtle temptations of Satan and will be seduced by the quest for power. But though God knew of man's fall in advance, He did not cause it; for He says that man will fall of his own volition.

The rebellious angels fell through pride; man shall fall by the same cause. But Milton is also careful to put into this speech God's assurance of grace to rescue man from the results of the fall— though the angels of Satan will have no such grace. Even before man chose to disobey God, Milton says, the mechanics for his salvation were in motion. Paul summed it up well: "For as in Adam all die, even so in Christ shall all be made alive" (I Cor. 15:22).

16

Book VII of *Paradise Lost* tells of the glorious process of creation: from the forming of light on the first day to the wondrous appearance of man on the sixth. Man differs from the rest of creation; he is, John Milton tells us, "not prone and brute as other creatures, but endu'd with sanctity of reason." Among man's tasks are the governing of the rest of creation and the corresponding with heaven. But the poet emphasizes yet another and more important duty; "gratefully to acknowledge whence his good descends thither with heart and voice and eyes directed in devotion, to adore and worship God supreme who made him chief of all his works."

How far we have come from that sense of devotion! Modern man has all but forgotten how to call on God's name except in profanity, or except in extreme emergency—as though God were an ambulance service. Man's chief desire should be to please God and to acknowledge Him as the Source of all wisdom, strength, power, and knowledge. But this has been superseded by a humanistic viewpoint which says that "man is the measure of all things" and that God's part in human affairs is, at best, incidental. Even Adam and Eve, who had no precedent to follow (except, perhaps, Satan and his cohorts) soon discovered the seductive attraction of exercising their independence from God. As a result, they drowned out the music of the spheres with the cacophony of their own wills.

One of the most difficult tasks Milton forged for himself in *Paradise Lost* was not the description of creation, as complex as that was, nor the fight in heaven between the forces of Satan and the forces of God, as dramatic as that was. Rather, it is the description of Adam and Eve immediately after their sin, because (as with all sin) the ultimate results were interior; yet the poet had to make these results evident.

Here is the passage that tells what happened to the first sinners:

> They sat them down to weep, not only tears
> Rain'd at their eyes, but high winds worse within
> Began to rise, high passions, anger, hate,
> Mistrust, suspicion, discord, and shook sore
> Their inward state of mind, calm region once
> And full of peace, now toss't and turbulent;
> For understanding rul'd not, and the Will
> Heard not her lore, both in subjection now
> To sensual appetite, who from beneath
> Usurping over sovran reason claim'd
> Superior sway.

How sad and pitiful is this! That marvelous creation, made in the image of God Himself (incapable of blemish or flaw) has now, by its own choice, become subject to such unpleasant—and fatal—consequences. One act of sin, as harmless as it may have seemed, has brought horror in its wake. As he did with Adam and Eve, Satan likes nothing better than to make us believe that what we are doing is in our best interests, whether or not God is served. However, after he has convinced us to eat of the forbidden fruit, he will inevitably crawl off, leaving us exposed in our own nakedness.

The expulsion of Adam and Eve from the Garden of Eden after their sin of disobedience is a matter of biblical record. In the last two books of *Paradise Lost,* Milton has Michael the Archangel come down to Adam and Eve to soften the blow of their punishment by giving them a glimpse into the future. As Adam and Eve watch, Michael reveals to them Cain's murder of Abel, the flood, the tower of Babel, the coming of Abraham (beginning the history of God's people) and of Isaac, the adventures of Joseph and of Moses. Finally, with a note of triumph, the great warrior-angel brings the vision to the coming of Christ and gives Adam words of comfort.

It is very doubtful, of course, that Adam really knew how God intended to offset the results of his sin—this section in Milton's epic is purely poetic license. It is likely, however, that Adam had some assurance, some idea of God's benevolence toward His creation. Here we have what medieval scholars called the "paradox of the fortunate fall," which says that if Adam had never sinned, we never would have known firsthand the glories of Christ and His redeeming grace. This position is debatable; we will leave the question to theologians. We can be sure of one thing, however. When Adam sinned, the love which had caused creation was sufficient also to cause a remedy, to spawn the ultimate solution to man's sinful inheritance. The great paradox of the age is that the only barrier to the effectiveness of God's antidote to sin is man's failure to recognize that although "in Adam all die, even so in Christ shall all be made alive" (I Cor. 15:22).

Many legends survive about the magnificent oratorio, Handel's *Messiah*. Handel reportedly stayed in his house for twenty-four days to complete the music; he found little reception in London and so went to Dublin for the premiere performance; King George II, profoundly moved by the emotion of the Hallelujah Chorus, stood to his feet, a tradition which persists today. The *Messiah* was first performed in 1742, and Handel's fame grew from that time.

The libretto, drawn entirely from Scripture, is divided into three parts: God's plan to redeem mankind; the redemption; and thanksgiving. The first part is further divided into "the promise" and "the realization." Old Testament words, mostly from Isaiah, first show the promise given to a people in travail, seriously needing the Messiah: "Comfort ye, comfort ye, my people." But the Messiah's coming is not to be tranquil, for we hear these warnings: "Thus saith the Lord of hosts . . . I will shake the heavens, and the earth, the sea and the dry land. . . . But who may abide the day of His coming?" (No wonder the manger so effectively disguised the Messiah's arrival!) The "promise" section ends with imagery of light, showing His impact on the lives of the waiting ones: "Arise, shine; for thy light is come, and the glory of the Lord is risen upon thee. . . . The Gentiles shall come to thy light. . . . The people that walked in darkness have seen a great light."

The "realization" section relates gospel accounts to prophecy, referring to Christ's healing: "Then shall the eyes of the blind be opened, and the ears of the deaf unstopped..." and to His comforting: "He shall feed his flock like a shepherd... for He is meek and lowly of heart," ending with the assurance that "His yoke is easy, and His burden is light."

And this is only the beginning—the simple yet terribly awesome process of God keeping His promise.

20

After showing God's plan to redeem mankind, and its fulfillment by the coming of Christ, the final part of Handel's *Messiah* turns to the future.

The Scripture first rendered is the incandescent vision of Job in the midst of his travail: "I know that my Redeemer liveth, and that He shall stand at the latter day upon the earth." Then comes the assurance from Paul to the Corinthian church that at the end of things the trumpet shall sound: "We shall all be changed . . . in the twinkling of an eye," for "this corruption must put on incorruption and this mortal must put on immortality." This is the often unacknowledged promise of the incarnation: eternal life, rescue from the creeping blight of deterioration to which the flesh is subject.

Handel concludes this section, and the oratorio, with the full chorus singing a section of Revelation chapter five: "Worthy is the Lamb that was slain, and hath redeemed us to God by His blood, to receive power, and riches, and wisdom, and strength, and honor, and glory and blessing." This is the great and powerful beauty of the Christmas message.

21

One of the strengths of poetry is its ability to condense great ideas or universal thoughts into a small space. The subject of death and its inevitability, for instance, has a bittersweet attraction for most people. We do not like to talk about our own death, and yet we all have a touch of morbidity which draws us to accident sites or causes us to read the obituaries.

Poets, too, have long been fascinated with the end of life. Perhaps the most famous poem on this subject is, in fact, set in a cemetery. In "Elegy in a Country Churchyard," Thomas Gray is especially eloquent about the leveling nature of death:

> The boast of heraldry, the pomp of power,
> And all that beauty, all that wealth e'er gave
> Awaits alike the inevitable hour:
> The paths of glory lead but to the grave.

Christians may, like other men, fear dying. But there is a basic difference: believers *need not* be afraid of death. We have a great number of assurances—from Psalm 23 to Paul's affirmations in I Corinthians 15 to the Revelation of John—that death is neither a solitary nor a terminal experience. We know, even if the poet had not told us, that neither fame, wealth, nor power can rescue us from the "inevitable hour." But that hour can be, praise God, the beginning of a path of glory leading *from* the grave.

The world is too much with us; late and soon,
Getting and spending, we lay waste our powers:
Little we see in Nature that is ours;
We have given our hearts away, a sordid boon!

Wordsworth's lament here echoes the age-old warning of prophets from Jonah to John the Baptist against the seductive poison of materialism. Man has always been attracted most by what his senses tell him will bring him the highest pleasure or the quickest quenching of his desires. Wordsworth's concern here is that modern man's preoccupation with possessions will cause him to ignore the loveliness of nature. In the Old Testament, spiritual greed caused God's people to ignore truth; this problem was at the root of the building of the golden calf, and the many episodes of unfaithfulness to Jehovah.

Most Christians do not feel called to the ascetic life of the monastery to combat the contemporary preoccupation with "getting and spending." On the other hand, there is a calculated danger in following the practice of our culture. In matters of the Spirit, the majority is seldom right; its decisions are based on expediency. We have only one heart to give away; let us choose wisely where we invest it. If we want God's approval, let us exercise our sense of spiritual ecology and avoid the promiscuous "laying waste of our powers."

23

Some poems are difficult to understand because they have meanings on many levels. Samuel Taylor Coleridge's "The Rime of the Ancient Mariner" is one of these. The poem tells the story of a sailor who capriciously shoots an albatross (a good-luck omen), and for that foolish act his shipmates force him to wear the dead bird around his neck.

What does this mean? What is the significance of the sailor's deed and his punishment? Most scholars agree that the mariner had broken a trust with nature, that by spilling innocent blood he had violated the sanctity of life.

After several bizarre visions, the mariner sees water snakes playing in the sea, and he suddenly feels for them a love he has not known for many days. As he blesses them for their beauty, the albatross falls off "like lead into the sea." As part of the lingering curse, however, the mariner must carry the burden of his story across the face of the earth. Whenever he stops to tell it, those who listen are spellbound, and stay to hear in spite of themselves.

There are many parallels between the story of the ancient mariner and that of the redeemed Christian: both have done wrong and both are chastened for their errant deeds. But there is an essential difference: the mariner, though he lost the weight of the albatross, still was cursed to wander; he could never be still or calm in his heart.

The redeemed man, on the other hand, has had his sin taken from him "as far as the east is from the west." When the Christian tells his story, it is not one of driven compulsion but rather is a triumphant tale of freedom and the glory of delivery.

24

By the shimmering clear waters of Lake Geneva in eastern Switzerland stands the Castle of Chillon. It is a magnificent medieval chateau, affording its many visitors a beautiful view of the lake and the surrounding mountains. But the Castle of Chillon is more than a tourist attraction, more than a remnant of the days of knights and battles in mountain passes. It has become a monument to human freedom. Lord Byron, a frequent visitor to those parts, immortalized the castle when he wrote about the imprisonment of François de Bonivard (1496–1570).

Bonivard and his two brothers were imprisoned at Chillon in the sixteenth century because they differed with the state on religious matters. Byron's *Prisoner of Chillon*, written in the first person, gives Bonivard an opportunity to describe their plight:

> They chain'd us each to a column stone,
> And we were three—yet, each alone;
> We could not move a single pace,
> We could not see each other's face,
> ....
> Fetter'd in hand, but join'd in heart.

First one brother died and then the other. Bonivard found himself alone, his kindred buried under the very floor he walked on. But he rejected suicide, with the same conviction which had brought him to prison at the beginning:

> I had no earthly hope but faith,
> And that forbade a selfish death.

Through the dark months which followed the death of his brothers, Bonivard found little to sustain himself, until one day

> A light broke in upon my brain—
> It was the carol of a bird;
> . . . .
>
> But then by dull degrees came back
> My senses to their wonted track;
> . . . .
>
> And it was to come to love me when
> None lived to love me so again,
> And cheering from my dungeon's brink
> Had brought me back to feel and think.

To think that the worst torment and punishment man could contrive could be so effectively reversed by the song of a bird! This is Byron's way of praising the unquenchable spirit of man and his feeling of comradeship with the "lesser" creatures of God's handiwork. It is this very "spirit of the chainless mind" that Byron writes about in a prefatory sonnet which speaks of man's eternal quest for liberty that is, the poet tells us, "brightest in dungeons."

On one of his visits to Chillon, Byron carved his name in one of "the seven pillars of Gothic mould," which the modern visitor may enjoy still. It might well have been on the same visit that the poet was moved enough by the lingering presence of Bonivard to return to his study and write these words of tribute:

Chillon! thy prison is a holy place,
And thy sad floor an altar—for 'twas trod,
Until his very steps have left a trace
Worn, as if thy cold pavement were a sod,
By Bonivard! May none these marks efface!
For they appeal from tyranny to God.

25

Nathaniel Hawthorne (1804–1864) was the New England literary master with the haunted conscience. The moral dilemmas of his "tales" (the term *short story* came later) consistently trapped his characters; the themes were profoundly symbolic.

One such story is "The Birthmark," which tells of a great scientist who married a stunningly beautiful woman. She had just one small physical flaw—a slight birthmark on the side of her face. The husband became obsessed with the desire to remove the blemish. In his laboratory he finally found the right combination of chemicals. His wife drank the potion, and it began to take effect—the birthmark became lighter and lighter, until it was almost invisible. Then, just as the blemish faded completely, the young woman gasped and stopped breathing. The scientist-husband had achieved his end, but had lost something far more precious in the process.

The birthmark was far more than a birthmark. It was a symbol of its bearer's humanity, the badge of her uniqueness. But her husband was blind to this and killed her with his homemade salvation.

God has blessed each of us with unique characteristics, and we should not repress them. Although striving for perfection is laudable and scriptural, perfection will not be gained until we reach heaven. In the meantime, to deny what makes us peculiarly human is to second-guess God's judgment.

Robert Browning is known primarily for his courtship of Elizabeth Barrett, the sickly poetess of Wimpole Street; his love of the Italian Renaissance; and his use of the dramatic monologue to create individual characters of great strength and personality.

Another important, though less-known, dimension to Browning's work was his great optimism. He encouraged all to continue to grow, to expand themselves, to stretch beyond what they thought possible. Of the dozens of passages from Browning's poetry dealing with this need for individual growth, one of the clearest comes in "Bishop Blougram's Apology":

> When the fight begins within himself,
> A man's worth something. God stoops o'er his head,
> Satan looks up between his feet—both tug—
> He's left, himself, i' the middle: the soul wakes
> And grows. Prolong that battle through his life!
> Never leave growing till the life to come!

This is parallel to the scriptural advice to "continue in the way" or to "grow in grace" or to "fight the good fight." This idea of struggle is very real for most people, who continually face difficulties ranging from money problems to sickness to family conflicts. The Bible declares that every experience, no matter how dark or painful, ought to contribute to our growth and to our understanding of the working of God in our lives.

The ability to cope ought to be a peculiarly Christian strength; a Christian recognizes that there is a pattern in the tapestry, the hand of God is indeed present in what seems to be a muddle, and His light is in the midst of the darkness. As Browning says, the struggle in which we are perpetually engaged can be won if we will lend ourselves to growth. We do this by making ourselves vulnerable to divine leadership, and by aspiring to those heights which in ourselves would be impossible to attain. Thus Browning reminds us that

> A man's reach should exceed his grasp,
> Or what's a heaven for?

27

Alfred Tennyson, poet laureate of England for forty-two years, is conceived by many scholars as the embodiment of the Victorian period in literature. Much of his best poetry is elegiac, celebrating the tragically premature death of his close friend, Arthur Hallam, at the age of twenty-two. The central poem of these, *In Memoriam,* is also one of the most important poems of the nineteenth century.

In the hundreds of lines which make up this chronicle, the poet-speaker goes through an intellectual, emotional, and spiritual evolution concerning his friend's life and death, the matter of immortality, and the cruel necessity of sorrow.

When he started the poem, Tennyson was reluctant to share his deep grief in such a public way. As he says, "I sometimes hold it half a sin/ To put in words the grief I feel;/ For words, like Nature, half reveal/ And half conceal the Soul within." But as time passed and Tennyson continued the poem, he was able to admit the value of his friendship with Hallam despite the sudden loss (this recognition is marked by the "Christmas stanzas"). In lines misquoted and badly used over the years, but very sensitive nonetheless, he states a universal truth which those who experience deep loss can affirm: "I hold it true, whate'er befall;/ I feel it, when I sorrow most;/ 'Tis better to have loved and lost/ Than never to have loved at all."

Tennyson's realization of the value of love—even love terminated by separation, loss, and death—was a long time coming and an important lesson to absorb. Genuine love always edifies and enhances, for in loving we participate in an activity ordained for us from the beginning of time. Though cruelly torn asunder by circumstance, love remains an invaluable possession, undiminished by time or a loved one's death. Since love ultimately flows from God the eternal, the poet is right: better to know it for a season than to miss its loveliness completely.

28

One of Tennyson's lesser known poems is "Tithonus," the lament of a mortal who became the beloved of the goddess of the dawn, Aurora. He received from her as a wedding gift the right to live eternally, but, alas, without the eternal youth with which to enjoy his perpetual life.

At the beginning of the poem, Tithonus is extremely old, but has no prospect of dying. He looks around him and sees the cycle of life and death everywhere—everywhere, that is, except in his own life: "The woods decay, the woods decay and fall,/ The vapors weep their burden to the ground,/ Man comes and tills the field and lies beneath,/ And after many a summer dies the swan." The speaker realizes he is out of step with the natural order and that his immortality is a burden, not a blessing.

Since the Tower of Babel, man has desired to suspend or alter the natural order of things, especially if it could contribute to his own feelings of self-importance. Like Tithonus, however, man has found that the results of such efforts are less than satisfying. Time and time again he has been forced to admit that the original conception, the Creator's intention, was the better way after all.

Of course, this does not reflect on the many scientific and technological discoveries which have been made in the past centuries. Rather it applies to those efforts, both private and collective, which contradict rather than improve the order of things.

It is unfortunate that Tithonus, on the eve of his marriage, could not have had a brief conversation with the writer of Ecclesiastes, who would have reminded him that for "everything there is a season." Even death has its season; if one tries to stick his puny hand in the great flywheel of God's creation, the consequences will be painful.

Just a few days before his death in 1892, Tennyson instructed that whenever his poems were col-
lected, in however small a number, "Crossing the
Bar" should always appear last. This short poem
is often seen on printed pamphlets provided by
funeral directors to indicate the deceased person's
birthdate, place of burial, and so on. It is not a
particularly good poem, but has come to stand as
an optimistic statement of the meaning of death.

The metaphor used by the poet is that of a voyage out of the familiar harbor, past the bar (the
sand bar which marks the beginning of open
ocean). It is evening, as might be expected, and
the poet speaks of hearing a "clear call" but asks
that there be no "sadness of farewell" when he
embarks. The reason for this remarkable courage
is not found, interestingly enough, in the
speaker's confidence of where the voyage will
end. Rather, as the last two lines reveal, it is found
in the fact that aboard his vessel from the beginning has been the Pilot (explained by Tennyson as
that "divine and unseen who is always guiding
us"), whom he will now see "face to face."

With all the weaknesses of the poem, structural
and rhetorical, there is one distinct message at
which we ought to cast at least a sidelong glance.
Tennyson does not pretend to know his destination; he does not speculate on the nature of the
hereafter. What he does do is to depend on the
presence of the Pilot, whom the Christian reader

would acknowledge as Christ the Lord, to steer him through the buoys and away from the rocks to the final destination.

Let us so live that when we breathe our last, we will, with the poet, be able to stare with confidence into that utter darkness which lies beyond the bar. As Christians, we know that He who walked the waters of Galilee can surely guide us to the port where the mansions that He has prepared for us dominate the skyline.

30

How dangerous it is to be satisfied with things as they are. Tennyson, the great (though now-neglected) Victorian poet, conveyed this message in a fine poem about Ulysses, the ancient warrior and victorious general in the Trojan Wars. Tennyson's Ulysses is an old man who has been relegated to a rocking-chair throne—and he does not like it! In this dramatic monologue we hear him making plans to sail away again. He does not know where he will sail, but sail he will, for he is dissatisfied with merely existing. He says, as we listen: "I am a part of all that I have met;/ Yet all experience is an arch wherethrough/ Gleams that untraveled world whose margin fades/ Forever and forever when I move."

What a magnificent insight this reveals! The image of the fading margin shows the hero's recognition that each new adventure can serve to broaden horizons and expand life's meaning.

But there are even greater observations by the aging king: "How dull it is to pause, to make an end,/ To rust unburnished, not to shine in use!/ As though to breathe were life! Life piled on life/ Were all too little, and of one to me/ Little remains; but every hour is saved/ From that eternal silence, something more,/ A bringer of new things...." This is the attitude for an invigorating and rewarding life. Ulysses admits that he is not sure what is ahead, but he is not concerned. He is pledged to action, to throwing himself into the

59

sheer activity of living. As he says at the end of the poem, his heart has been "made weak by time and fate, but strong in will/ To strive, to seek, to find, and not to yield."

God created us to live fully and abundantly—not to give up the race before the finish line is in sight. Those who are most content are those who know that they have spent every ounce of their strength and every minute of their time living as God intended them to live. The example of the speaker in Tennyson's poem is paralleled by the wonderful testimony of the apostle Paul (in II Tim. 4) who knew that he had "fought a good fight," that he had "finished [his] course," and also knew—though the pagan Ulysses could only hope for this—that a divine and eternal reward awaited him: "henceforth there is laid up for me a crown of righteousness."

31

From the time of Moses' visit to the top of Sinai, the Ten Commandments, also known as the Decalogue, have been at the very heart of the biblical ethic—the standard for moral and spiritual behavior.

A little more than a century ago, an English poet named Arthur Hugh Clough wrote a poem called "The Latest Decalogue." He gave the old laws a modern twist, and declaimed them as he saw them being lived in the prosperity of the mid-Victorian period. Expediency now has become the measure of all things, says Clough; men still have only one God, for "who would be at the expense of two?" The only graven image allowed now to be worshiped is the currency; the attendance of church on Sunday will "serve to keep thee thy friend"; one is to honor one's parents—at least those parents "from whom advancement may befall."

This is not merely cynicism on Clough's part. The 1860s were not a time of great piety; the British Isles were the center of the greatest industrial and political power the world had ever seen, and it was thought by those basking in the glory of the British Empire that man was needful of only an occasional nudge from the divine.

Clough continues his poetic observation: though the law says, "Thou shalt not kill," modern man has decided that he "need'st not strive officiously to keep alive"; that adultery ought not to be committed since "the lie will have time on its own wings to fly." Clough finishes his examination of modern values by saying: "The sum of all it, thou shalt love,/ If anybody, God above:/ At any rate shall never labor/ More than thyself to love thy neighbor."

Clough here perceptively observes that nothing is sacred. He laments that the law God wrote with His own hand has become obscured and diluted, transcribed as it is in modern man's troubled hieroglyphic.

Charles Dicken's life was not a happy one. The celebrated novelist was reared in poverty, and his mind and psyche were scarred early. His father was imprisoned for debt, and he had to work in a dreary factory—while other boys his age were in school, learning things young Charles could only dream about. Partly because he was jilted by his first love, his attitude toward women and marriage throughout his life was not a positive one. Eventually he came to the point where he could not tolerate the sight of his own wife. He had severe arguments with publishers over money, and alienated Americans by unflattering remarks about his visits to the United States. His last years were filled with traveling to and from lecture halls, where he gave oral readings from his works. Indeed, his schedule was frenetic; he seemed driven by demons within until his death in 1870 at the age of 58.

Yet Dickens wrote some of the most sympathetic and tender works in English literature; his portrayal of childhood has seldom been paralleled. He described the plights of Oliver Twist, David Copperfield (a fictional depiction of Dickens's own life), Little Nell, Philip Pirrup (better known as "Pip"), Paul Dombey, and Jo, the crossing sweeper. These children's hard and often sorrow-filled lives were the result of social and moral injustices in nineteenth-century England. The children were fictionalized but the injustices and excesses described were not; the hurts Dickens suffered as a child were reflected in his books and echoed in his satires, motivated by an anger that could not be quelled.

A close study of his books, even a story as well known as *A Christmas Carol,* shows that Dickens often hoped for the redemption of man—but doubted it would occur. He catalogued the dangers of his time, but was without a solution to counteract them. Because of this, the demon that drove him to write with such energy and zeal could never be chased away or laid to rest. For all his genius, Charles Dickens never knew that the answer to earthly ills was nowhere to be found on earth.

I believe a leaf of grass is no less than the journey-work
    of the stars,
And the pismire is equally perfect, and a grain of sand,
    and the egg of the wren,
And the tree-toad is a chef-d'oevre for the highest,
And the running blackberry would adorn the parlors of
    heaven,
And the narrowest hinge in my hand puts to scorn all
    machinery,
And the cow crunching with depressed head surpasses
    any statue,
And a mouse is miracle enough to stagger sextillions of
    infidels.

This rhapsodic song of praise was written by Walt Whitman, the Camden, New Jersey, poet who was years ahead of his time. With that magnificent vision given to poets, he saw the wonders of nature, the handiwork of God, and its superiority to man's best accomplishments. Note that Whitman does not focus on the Grand Canyon or the ruby-throated hummingbird or the polar bear or any other of God's showcase creations. He is sufficiently moved by grass and toads and blackberries and mice to affirm that the "common" world of nature has much to offer to the one who will stop to observe.

Whitman lived and wrote in the period after the Civil War, when factories, mines, and mills were working overtime to serve the needs of a growing population. Man's might was evident everywhere, with new products, bigger smokestacks, and greater machinery. In the midst of all this mechanistic grandeur, Whitman declares the great beauty of the natural, the elegance of the God-created. Take the lowliest animal you can think of, says Whitman—a mouse. There is enough of a miracle, enough of God's wonder in that small creature, to make a believer out of the most committed atheist. What Whitman saw, then, was a pattern in the world of nature, a systematic intervention from a Supernatural Source. This makes the lowliest thing grand, the homeliest beautiful; mere grains of sand and eggs of wren are beyond man's creative capability.

There is a lesson here for us. We live in a world even more sophisticated and technologically advanced than Whitman's, and there is an increased danger of our being blind to the grandeur of God. Take Whitman's advice: look at the perfect design of your hand and think of the magnificence of the One who made us.

The essayists of Victorian England were sometimes called "prophets" because of their doomsday rhetoric and strong warnings against creeping materialism. One of the most prolific of these essayists was Matthew Arnold, a man given to powerful statements about the emptiness of modern life.

Arnold was also a celebrated poet; in his most famous poem, "Dover Beach," he says that no matter how attractive and seductive the contemporary scene appears, there is less there than meets the eye:

> . . . for the world, which seems
> To lie before us like a land of dreams,
> So various, so beautiful, so new,
> Hath really neither joy, nor love, nor light,
> Nor certitude, nor peace, nor help for pain. . . .

Arnold is warning that appearances can be deceiving and the prosperity and novelty of the day are not enough. He has taken a look and found that the ingredients of *moral* prosperity are missing: "neither joy, nor love, nor light,/ Nor certitude, nor peace, nor help for pain. . . ."

England was then in the throes of the Industrial Revolution with its accompanying social upheaval. The British Empire was spreading around the globe, making its way across international borders with the strength of great armies. Yet this was a time in which happiness and concern for others or the light of truth—indeed, anything certain or concrete at all—was extremely rare.

Arnold's ability to penetrate to the core truth—as painful as that truth often is—is what makes him prophetic. He draws upon the past in a manner that speaks to his present, yet his words apply to our era as well. This is seen in the last three lines of "Dover Beach." Taking an image from ancient history, Arnold speaks of the uncertainty of his times in words that also fit today's situation:

And we are here as on a darkling plain
Swept with confused alarms of struggle and flight,
Where ignorant armies clash by night.

Christina Georgina Rossetti, the pious sister of the painter-poet Dante Gabriel Rossetti, wrote a hauntingly allegorical piece about the walk of life, its difficulties and its final triumph. The poem uses two voices, one which questions and one which answers. The poem begins in midcourse, perhaps as the weary travelers have paused a moment and looked upward:

DOES THE ROAD WIND UPHILL ALL THE WAY?
Yes, to the very end.
WILL THE DAY'S JOURNEY TAKE THE WHOLE
   LONG DAY?
From morn to night, my friend.
BUT IS THERE FOR THE NIGHT A RESTING-PLACE?
A roof for when the slow dark hours begin.
MAY NOT THE DARKNESS HIDE IT FROM MY FACE?
You cannot miss the inn.
SHALL I MEET OTHER WAYFARERS AT NIGHT?
Those who have gone before.
THEN MUST I KNOCK OR CALL WHEN JUST IN
   SIGHT?
They will not keep you standing at the door.
SHALL I FIND COMFORT, TRAVEL-SORE AND
   WEAK?
Of labor, you shall find the sum.
WILL THERE BE BEDS FOR ME AND ALL WHO SEEK?
Yes, beds for all who come.

How encouraging is this picture! We all know that our walk through life is uphill, but what a consolation it is to know there is a resting place "when the slow dark hours begin." And the idea that those who have traveled before us, those we often call "heroes of the faith," will be there when we arrive is delightful to contemplate. To rest and listen to the soothing music of the spheres and to the retelling of Martin Luther's story of his confrontation at Worms, or Wesley's account of that night at Aldersgate will be worth all the painful stumbles and travel-hazards of this upward walk.

36

Gerard Manley Hopkins is a poetic name with which all Christians need to be familiar. Hopkins was a Jesuit priest, and subordinated his poetry writing to his clerical duties. His true devotion to God was never discovered until his poetry was published many years after his quiet and anonymous death. It is obvious from his poems that Hopkins was overwhelmed by the presence of the Almighty; he was awestruck by the thought of the intervention of the Creator in the small affairs of men.

What a pity that we have lost this sense of mystery and wonder; we are a generation so calloused that few things move us, including the wonder of God stirring in His world. Hopkins's poem, "God's Grandeur," shows his unique poetic style which incorporates enjambment, instress, inscape, elliptical syntax, and other devices common to the modern, postmetrical poets. Remembering that poetry is best when it is read out loud (and Hopkins wrote to be read orally if any man ever did), read the following:

The world is charged with the grandeur of God.
It will flame out, like shining from shook foil;
It gathers to a greatness, like the ooze of oil
Crushed. Why do men then now not reck His rod?
Generations have trod, have trod, have trod;
And all is seared with trade; bleared, smeared with toil;
And wears man's smudge and shares man's smell: the
    soil
Is bare now, nor can foot feel, being shod.

And for all this, nature is never spent;
There lives the dearest freshness deep down things;
And though the last lights off the black West went
Oh, morning, at the brown brink eastward, springs—
Because the Holy Ghost over the bent
World broods with warm breast and ah! bright wings.

Hopkins acutely senses the immense discrepancy between the world as God originally intended and the world as man has "bleared, smeared with toil." We have, laments the speaker, lost the ability to experience the "freshness deep down things." That is to say, we have lost the sense of the "essence" of things, their origins, their flowing out of the hand of God.

Man rarely glimpses the ripe image with which Hopkins ends his paean of praise. Men forget God the Holy Spirit not because He has ceased to exist; rather, they have lowered their eyes and so grope through the fog of their own futile industries.

37

The literary career of Oscar Wilde is a fascinating subject, and is still controversial among literary historians—even eighty years after Wilde's death. His was a colorful life; he is remembered for his lecture-tour of America (including talks at the mining camps of Colorado holding a white lily in his hand); the morals trial and imprisonment at Reading Gaol; the magnificent cynicism of his play, *The Importance of Being Earnest*. All these and more make Wilde one of English literature's more memorable personalities.

Legend has it that in the course of his rising fame, Wilde was asked to sit for a portrait by a prominent artist. When the sittings were finished, Wilde looked at the portrait and commented, "What a tragic thing it is! The portrait shall never grow older, and I shall. If it was only the other way." This offhand remark was allegedly the germ which grew into one of Wilde's most important and exhilarating works, *The Picture of Dorian Gray*.

This gothic and chilling suspense tale is an account of a handsome, ambitious, ruthless man who acted without restraint of conscience. His great wish was that he retain the youth and good looks of his mid-twenties while the portrait of himself hanging on his drawing-room wall would grow older. As the years passed, his wish came true: he lived a fast and thoughtless life without a trace of age appearing on his face, while the expression of the figure in the portrait began to darken. Before long, the young man, whose friends complimented him on his perpetual youth, noticed that the painted man was becoming wrinkled, and he relegated the portrait to the farthest reaches of the attic.

Several years later, while looking for some lost object in the attic, the still-handsome Dorian Gray accidentally knocked the cover from his portrait. He stood face to face with his true self—warped, grotesque, and misfeatured nearly beyond recognition. The portrait reflected the cruelty and hedonism of Dorian Gray, and the impact of the degenerate life he had led. He had been deceiving himself by looking in a mirror which told him only what he wanted to know.

This story clearly reflects scriptural truths. While Oscar Wilde would hardly have intended to do so, he has in *The Picture of Dorian Gray* given a vivid application of Christ's parable of the salt which has lost its savor. The once useful and pure is now trodden under the foot of man (Matt. 5:13); the corrupt must be discarded and destroyed.

At the very end of the Victorian period of English literature—about 1895 to 1910—two kinds of poetry dominated the literary scene. The first kind had a "decadent" lyric which extolled the fleshly pastimes and the material nature of the world; the second, a strongly orthodox type (written mainly by Roman Catholics), stressed the necessity of allowing God's dominance in the believer's heart. Francis Thompson fit this second category. His masterpiece, "The Hound of Heaven," is known by generations of English students and ought to be known by all Christians.

The verse structure of "The Hound of Heaven" is irregular, and the poetic diction is unusual. Indeed, a strong message of rebellion is communicated by the unique form:

I fled Him, down the nights and down the days;
I fled Him, down the arches of the years;
I fled Him down the labyrinthine ways
Of my own mind; and in the mist of tears
I hid from Him, and under running laughter.
Up vistaed hopes I sped;
And shot, precipitated,
Adown titanic glooms of chasmed fears,
From those strong Feet that followed, followed after.

What a keenly accurate picture of modern man! How often has he sought refuge in the "labyrinthine ways of his own mind"? The streets of the cities are filled with people trying to hide "under running laughter" or "in the mist of tears." Man has always found dozens of alternatives to heeding the voice of God, and most of them have been dead-end streets of "vistaed hopes." But this is not the end of the story, for those "strong Feet" were persistent:

> But with unhurrying chase
> And unperturbed pace,
> Deliberate speed, majestic instancy,
> They beat—And a Voice beat
> More instant than the Feet—
> "All things betray thee, who betrayest Me."

And although the chase continues through most of the poem, the one pursued at last gives in to this "Hound of Heaven." He recognizes that running away to be free is really the worst sort of captivity—that true freedom can come only from surrender to Him who loves us enough to pursue us.

39

The novels of Thomas Hardy are chronicles of grief and defeat—at least the major ones fall into this category. *The Mayor of Casterbridge* is the story of a man who climbed to the top of the heap in business and in politics only to be brought down by his own excesses and lack of control. *Tess of the D'Urbervilles* tells of a young woman who has conceived and lost an illegitimate child. The burden of that fact follows her, interrupting her happiness, so that she is a prisoner of a past and an alien in her present. *Jude the Obscure* is even more depressing. Hardy begins with an idealistic young man who aspires to study and learn great things, but this promising scholar is eventually reduced to a bumbling sycophant who quotes rotely-learned Latin in pubs for six-pence. Jude Fawley dies, as he has lived, alone and forgotten.

Much has been written about why Thomas Hardy, an amiable little man at home among the rural customs and rustic folk of his native Dorset, has such a dark view of man's prospects. Some critics have traced in Hardy's writing a theme of fatalism, while others have said that Hardy was a product of his times, the end of the long, hidebound and rigid nineteenth century. Still others have concluded that Hardy's cloud-covered vision was at least partly the result of the superstitions of the local countryside.

Probably each of these theories is true to a degree, but there is a larger explanation why Hardy considered the maelstrom of destruction he wrote about simply a by-product of existence. Indeed, Hardy's vision itself was inadequate: there was no place in it for the possibility of a loving and caring Creator; rather, he assumed that "what will be, will be" is the most hopeful statement man can make.

This attitude, certainly exemplified in his major narrative tales, Hardy succinctly and poetically states thus:

> Let me enjoy the earth no less
> Because the all-enacting Might
> That fashioned forth its loveliness
> Had other aims than my delight.

If Hardy actually believed that—and there is no indication that such an attitude was simply a pose—he was clearly without an alternative in the literary direction he chose to take. He had to cut his heroes and heroines loose to fend for themselves in a world devoid of direction, sympathy, or the means to pick up the wanderer once he has fallen.

40

Thomas Hardy vehemently denied the frequent charge that he was a pessimist, or that his was a fatalistic view of life. He assumed that the state of the world and the plight of mankind reflected an indifference on the part of the Creator—if there had ever been one. Hardy felt that there must be some Power or Author of Order somewhere, but that He had long ago forgotten man. Consider his poem, "Hap," written when Hardy was in his mid-twenties:

> If but some vengeful god would call to me
> From up the sky, and laugh: "Thou suffering thing,
> Know that thy sorrow is my ecstasy,
> That thy love's loss is my hate's profiting!"
>
> Then would I bear it, clench myself, and die,
> Steeled by the sense of ire unmerited;
> Half-eased in that a Powerfuller than I
> Had willed and meted me the tears I shed.
>
> But not so. How arrives it joy lies slain,
> And why unblooms the best hope ever sown?
> —Crass Casualty obstructs the sun and rain,
> And dicing Time for gladness casts a moan....
> These purblind Doomsters had as readily strown
> Blisses about my pilgrimage as pain.

If this is not pessimism, it will serve adequately for our purposes. Here the author presumes that his unhappiness and misfortune are the result of random events, of mere chance. His life could have turned out happily as easily as it had turned out tragically. Hardy saw no predictability or logic in what happens to man, either collectively or individually. And he certainly saw no love or concern from an impersonal universe to one small mortal. If he could be assured, the narrator says, that the divine order actually opposed him, even undeservedly, he could at least comprehend some kind of purpose in the universe. But this is not so; the poet tells us we all suffer at the hands of a fickle and unsystematic destiny—characterized by those legendary blind sisters who spin the thread of life and then arbitrarily cut it.

It does not take a biblical scholar to know that the sentiments of this poem are in contradiction to the Holy Scriptures. The psalmist says that man has been made just a "little lower than the angels," and is the constant recipient of God's love and concern. Far from being ignored and forgotten by an anonymous absentee deity, the Bible tells us that even the number of hairs on our heads is known by God. We are assured that God sees the fallen sparrow, clothes the lilies of the field, and so much more will care for each of us.

41

In any evaluation of the spiritual dimension of Thomas Hardy's writings, mention should be made of the small glimmer of hope which appears from time to time in some of his poems. In a poem about Christmas (a season which will inspire hope if any will), Hardy at least admits the possibility of something better than we now know. In "The Oxen," the poet refers to the old folk legend which says that on every Christmas Eve, exactly at midnight, all the animals in the world kneel in silent worship of the Babe in the manger.

Hardy's narrator then describes the reaction he and his companions might have had on such an occasion:

> We pictured the meek mild creatures where
> They dwelt in their strawy pen,
> Nor did it occur to one of us there
> To doubt they were kneeling then.

But this is not Hardy's clearest declaration of optimism, for a few lines later the poet makes the matter a much more personal one;

> ... Yet, I feel,
> If someone said on Christmas Eve,
> "Come; see the oxen kneel,
> In the lonely barton by yonder coomb
> Our childhood used to know,"
> I should go with him in the gloom,
> Hoping it might be so.

One wonders how much of Hardy's life was spent "hoping it might be so." The general tenor of his literary works, in poems, novels, and tales, indicates that what hope he had was dried up by a darker and more prevalent vision of misery. Such a bleak vision not even the singing of angels and the kneeling of oxen could illuminate.

42

Regional poets are America's most overlooked literary resource. They write in the idiom of their own territory and use the imagery and the symbols of their native countryside. One of the most interesting and enduring of these localized verse-writers was Sidney Lanier, who lived and wrote in Brunswick, Georgia. Brunswick is a lovely coastal town made famous by General Oglethorpe and by the Wesleys and, in later days, by President Carter's visits.

Surrounding Brunswick on two sides are the picturesque Marshes of Glynn, which have become celebrated as the setting and title of Lanier's most famous work. Hidden in the lines of this movingly lyrical poem is a strong sense of God and the loveliness of His creation. Using the marsh and its flora and fauna, Lanier draws a beautiful analogy of his own experience with the Creator:

As the marsh-hen secretly builds on the watery sod,
Behold I will build me a nest on the greatness of God:
I will fly in the greatness of God as the marsh-hen flies
In the freedom that fills all the space 'twixt the marsh
    and the skies;
By so many roots as the marsh-grass sends in the sod
I will heartily lay me a-hold on the greatness of God.

If you visit Brunswick, you will see the oak tree under which it is said Lanier stood while writing "The Marshes of Glynn" (at the very least, he was probably inspired there). It is a lovely spot and still solitary enough to allow the modern-day visitor a sense of the vastness of the marshes and the "space 'twixt the marsh and the skies."

In this brief passage, Lanier speaks of three ways he senses the "greatness of God": building *on* it, flying *in* it, and laying *a-hold* on it. This recognition of a need for stability and support outside himself becomes the poet as much as does the beauty of his verse. Lanier's intimate communion with the marsh and its busy natural life had caused him to look beyond the grass and the birds to the Source of them all. In that wonderful moment the poet senses his need of the silent strength implicit in the life of the marsh, and longs for a sustaining portion of the "greatness of God."

Enthusiastic and vocal followers of God have often been given trouble by those who are less sensitive to divine motives or machinations. In George Bernard Shaw's play, *Saint Joan*, the familiar story of Joan of Arc is told with great emphasis placed on the opposition to Joan. Officials of the established church had become so politically motivated that they felt threatened when the real presence of God began to bring military victories and political optimism.

When the play begins, France is being attacked by English forces; the French people are filled with feelings of despair and defeat. Along comes a young woman named Joan, who claims that voices from heaven have sent her to lead the French armies to victory. In the opening scene, Joan asks the local official for a horse to go join the leaders of the army; but the official is too busy worrying about the hens that are not laying and the cows that are not producing. When, at the end of the scene, he finally relents and lets Joan have what she wants, the servant rushes in to say that now the hens are laying better than ever. This causes the official to admit that Joan "did come from God."

Joan's vision proves true, for she does lead the army to military triumph, and she succeeds in getting the Dauphin crowned King of France in Rheims Cathedral. But Joan soon runs into trouble, since she has done all of this with little regard for the generals, the cardinals, or the nobles. She knew her obligation was to God, and she allowed nothing to interfere with her calling. For her trouble she was burned at the stake.

But Shaw does not end his story there, for he brings Joan back twenty-five years after her execution to talk with those whom she had known. By this time, all the charges against her have been dropped, and a cross has been planned for the square where the burning stake once stood. But even then they are afraid of her, the purity of her conviction, the reality of her vision. Recognizing it is a fallen world in which God's ways are often unwelcome, Joan ends the play with a haunting question, "O God, that madest this beautiful earth, when will it be ready to receive Thy saints: How long, O Lord, how long?"

44

The American Civil War spawned several enduring pieces of literature which continue to re-
inforce determinations that such a tragedy never
again occur among the citizens of the United
States. Among the works which came out of that
era is the long narrative poem, *John Brown's
Body*, by Stephen Vincent Benet.

In the prelude to this epic work, Benet sets
down a dialogue between the captain of a slave
ship and his first mate. The captain is a New Eng-
lander, satisfied in the belief that the black
people being carried down deck are inferior. The
opening line is ironic, for it powerfully contradicts what follows:

> He closed the Bible carefully, putting it down
> As if his fingers loved it.

Yet it is this Bible-reading man who buys and
sells human beings like cattle; he is convinced the
Bible says "that the sons of Ham are to be
bondservants."

The captain had succeeded in separating his life
from his religion. He had read the Bible to say
what he wanted it to say: to justify his livelihood,
to affirm his spiritual myopia, to support his
wrongdoing. The smell which came from the
filthy conditions below deck symbolized the ran-
cidness of his whole enterprise.

This sort of rationalization is still very much
with us, if in much more subtle forms. We act

without discipline and live without restraint, and then look to the Bible to rescue us, to provide a stamp of approval for our questionable behavior. The Bible is intended as a light to cut the darkness; it is to be a guide, not an afterthought. Life and the Scripture are to be integrated and aligned; then only can we avoid the slave captain's tragic self-delusion.

45

It is sometimes difficult to understand the unequal disposition of material goods. The Scriptures teach that the prosperity of the wicked is temporary, but it is hard to keep this in perspective. Though fully devoted to God, many believers are struggling to feed and clothe their families, while those who make their living in dubious or sinful ways seem to be well insulated by wealth.

But, after all, it is an imperfect world, and all creation is groaning under the burdens of evil and injustice (Rom. 8:22). But believers know that "all flesh is as grass" (I Peter 1:24); only the spiritually short-sighted will trade their souls for a short-term profit. As Jesus asked, "For what shall it profit a man, if he shall gain the whole world, and lose his own soul? Or what shall a man give in exchange for his soul?" (Mark 8:36, 37).

One can think of several literary examples in connection with this theme of "the prosperity of the wicked." There is, for instance, the tragic world of F. Scott and Zelda Fitzgerald reflected in his novels, *The Great Gatsby* and *Tender Is the Night*, and in her lonely piece, *Save Me the Waltz*. The Fitzgeralds were the glittering people of their day, doyens of that period between wars when the world was on a perpetual and catastrophic binge.

During what Fitzgerald himself christened the "Jazz Age," a crowd of talented but pagan artists and writers rambled from region to region, sometimes from country to country, seeking some solace, some quenching for the persistent parching in their souls. As Jay Gatsby failed to find satisfaction in his magnificent mansion, though he gave extravagant parties and surrounded himself with hordes of people, so Fitzgerald, Gatsby's creator, never found the rest he longed for, though he lit up the literary skies with his brilliant writing about despairing men and women.

Zelda had a series of nervous breakdowns and finally died in a fire in a sanitarium for alcoholics. Scott died in Hollywood, at the end of his life no closer to that vision which had eluded him through a shattered marriage and years of indulgent living. His literary genius had manifested itself in the form of characters and stories stamped in his own clay-hearted image. "The withering flower," the image St. Peter uses to symbolize man's frailty, is an apt description of the Fitzgeralds' life, and the temporal beauty they pursued in the end turned to ashes.

46

The small town has long held a cherished place in American literature. There is Sinclair Lewis's *Main Street*, the story of frustrated dreams in the midwest; Sherwood Anderson's *Winesburg, Ohio*, the chronicle of unfulfilled dreams in rural Ohio; Thornton Wilder's *Our Town*, the delightful stage play about the daily routine in Grovers Corners, New Hampshire.

And then there is Edgar Lee Masters's *Spoon River Anthology*, a series of poetic epitaphs "spoken" from graves on a windy southern Illinois hillside. The dead now have nothing to lose by telling all, and their pitiful reminiscences and wrenching observations reveal the essence of the human condition. Here is all the indignation, frustration, anger, as well as the joy and delight of being alive. There are 244 speakers in the *Anthology*, each of them taking this one last opportunity given them by the poet to apologize, prophesy, and commiserate with those still alive. Most of all, they choose to philosophize and share the wisdom that the pure objectivity of death allows.

Some of the speakers are cynical, others bitter. But now and then we come to a gravesite from which the speaker articulates a softer understanding, a clearer perspective. Such a speaker is Marie Bateson, who sees something significant about the sculpture on her gravestone:

You observe the carven hand
With the index finger pointing heavenward.

That is the direction, no doubt.
But how shall one follow it?
It is well to abstain from murder and lust.
To forgive, do good to others, worship God
Without graven images.
But these are external means, after all,
By which you chiefly do good to yourself.
The inner kernel is freedom.
It is light, purity—
I can no more.
Find the goal or lose it, according to your vision.

The "vision" of which Marie speaks is, apparently, an individual experience. As with Isaiah in the temple or Jacob sleeping with his head on a rock, our true vision will come when our thoughts and attention are lifted in the direction indicated by that skillfully carved finger on Marie Bateson's grave.

47

It is curious how literary reputations come and go. The novelist who was popular in one decade is sometimes forgotten in the next; the playwright whose works were the rage in one period may be unread years later as tastes and attitudes change. One of the American writers whose reputation has taken a plunge and whose words are now largely considered period pieces is Sinclair Lewis. Lewis was lionized in his day, winning the Nobel Prize for literature in 1930; his books were at the top of the best-seller lists and were awaited with great excitement as they appeared.

Lewis was the product of the prairies—he was born in Sauk Center, Minnesota—and as one biographer tells us, was always "a queer boy, always an outsider, lonely." He was tall, awkward, and red-haired—distinguishing features all—and never completely chased away that specter from his childhood: he was always an outsider. This perhaps explains why he is best known as a satirist, a creator of sensitive and misunderstood people who confront hypocrisy and materialism.

Lewis's best-known works are *Main Street*, a tale of his native Minnesota and an anatomy of that provincial society; *Babbitt*, a novel whose main character gave his name to the English language as the symbol of the tepid values and weak morality current between the wars; and *Arrowsmith*, the story of a doctor-*cum*-scientist's value struggle. These novels spoke to an America ripe for Lewis's brand of satire. He held a mirror to the dancing country and showed it its shortcomings and what it would cost to pay the fiddler.

One of the cruelest ironies is that Lewis himself paid a great price; like Fitzgerald and Faulkner, Lewis fell prey to the bottle, and that genius which had taken him to Stockholm to receive the world's most prestigious literary award was drowned in the bubbles of a thousand gin fizzes.

Sinclair Lewis was a true son of America, and is an important part of our literary tradition. He saw the dangers of modern Gomorrah, but could not resist the temptation of pitching his own tent in the midst of the flames.

48

In 1919, Sherwood Anderson published *Winesburg, Ohio,* a series of loosely connected stories about the eccentrics, or "grotesques," as the author calls them, in a small midwestern town. Each of the characters Anderson creates has his or her "moment," a brief interlude of insight and understanding. The tragedy of Anderson's people is that they seldom, if ever, recapture that moment of revelation, though they spend the rest of their lives trying to do so.

Among the emotional cripples Anderson writes about is Wing Biddlebaum, who was "forever frightened and beset by a ghostly band of doubts." Biddlebaum had been a teacher who loved his students, until an ugly rumor was started. The sensitive young schoolmaster was chased out of town and disappeared into tragic and isolated oblivion.

Then there was Dr. Reefy, who never opened windows, wore the same suit of clothes for ten years, and wrote messages on little papers, which he rolled into little balls and stuffed in his pockets. When the young woman Dr. Reefy married died, he sat in his empty office and watched the world pass him by.

The list goes on. There is Alice Hindman, a young woman who longs for love but finds no one who cares for her; the Rev. Curtis Hartman, who, while praying, sees the shadow of a woman in the adjoining house and has difficulty remembering what his true mission is; and Elizabeth Willard, the mother of the story's hero, who wanted to be an actress but lived and died with a dried-up box of stage makeup in her room. These are all God's children seen through the eyes of one man. This, said Anderson, is life as it is, not life as we want it.

And Anderson was right. Man has not done well with the gifts given him; more people are unhappy than are happy. While the "grotesques" in *Winesburg, Ohio* might seem exaggerated, the truth is that they are tame compared to what actually goes on in our communities. Man is alone and isolated because he has chosen to go his own way, and to ignore the admonitions and appeals of the One who made him.

49

Galesburg, Illinois, is a quintessentially midwestern town, its skyline dominated by a grain elevator and its afternoon air filled with the sound of trains. The people who live there are products of the prairie; independent, strong, and fiercely proud of their way of life.

Hidden on a side street on the edge of town is a modest home, not much different from others around it, and certainly not elaborate by today's standards. In this house was born one of America's great poets, Carl Sandburg, and it was here in the spacious backyard that he chose to be buried.

Visiting Sandburg's birthplace and learning of his humble origins (his father was a Swedish railwayman) leads us to wonder: what are the ingredients of genius? What was in the windblown prairies of western Illinois that played the right tune in Sandburg's psyche to turn him into a great writer?

One partial answer may be that he was born with all the ingredients—genius is a gift from God. This is why he could become our eyes and ears, writing so that we too would see and hear things clearly. If he had lived a few miles farther west, along the Mississippi, he might have written about boys whitewashing fences and growing up to be riverboat pilots; if he had been a product of the deep south, he might have concentrated on the breakup of the old social order.

But he was a product of the midwest prairies.

He gave us the great study of Lincoln, those marvelous *Rootabaga Stories* for children, and his poems of powerful imagery and perception. He captured the feel of the great midwest and made it accessible to readers in every land.

Carl Sandburg was a son of the prairies, but even more convincingly, he was a child of God. He had been given a rare gift of expression by God, and used that gift and vision to inspire us all to deeper understanding.

Robert Frost captures the essence of rural New England as few men have ever done. Using the imagery and locales of the countryside, Frost introduces us to moments, emotions, and characters which are both regional and universal, both highly individual and deeply rooted in general human experience.

In his familiar "The Road Not Taken," Frost describes a decision made in the past which had great implications for the speaker's future. The choice was a simple one—a choice between two roads, or paths. The speaker in the poem acknowledges he "could not travel both and be one traveler," so he deliberately started down one which "was grassy and wanted wear."

The speaker admits the decision was not an easy one, and confesses to experiencing pangs of uncertainty—which caused him to keep "the first [road] for another day." But while he admits his ambivalence, the speaker also realizes that the decision was permanent and that "knowing how way leads on to way, / I doubted if I should ever come back." He also recognizes that his decision has far-reaching, even eternal implications, so he ends his poem: "I shall be telling this with a sigh/ Somewhere ages and ages hence:/ Two roads diverged in a wood, and I—/ I took the one less traveled by,/ And that has made all the difference."

It would be difficult to give a specific interpretation of the elements of this poem; even Frost refused to reveal the exact meaning. To say, for instance, that the two roads certainly represent the narrow and broad ways of which Jesus spoke is to limit the poem unnecessarily. But this is one of the wonderful things about poetry; it is flexible enough to fit the contours of experience. We can agree that God in His wisdom has given us a great number of decisions to make—some trivial and transitory, others vital and eternal. Often the choice "less traveled by" is the hardest to make, but it is also often the one which "makes all the difference."

Robert Frost is the master of the purposely un-
clear, deliberately ambiguous statement. What, for
instance, does he mean when he closes one of his
poems with the line, "One could do worse than be
a swinger of birches?"

Obviously, the context of the entire poem must
be used to decipher this remark. The theme of the
poem "Birches" is one close to the poet's heart:
the purity of the rural setting, and the clear light
that comes from pursuing the simple life. The
speaker is set off on his remarks by the sight of
some bent birch trees. While he supposes they
were damaged in an ice storm, he wants to imagine they were bent by a farm boy, "too far from
town to learn baseball," who played there "as he
went out and in to fetch the cows." The speaker
would have us know that swinging birches cor-
rectly is no easy thing; it takes great skill to keep
one's balance and poise.

Just as we are wondering at the seriousness with
which the speaker is taking this seemingly trivial
pastoral pastime, the truth leaps out at us: "So was
I once myself a swinger of birches./ And so I
dream of going back to be." The innocent tree-
swinging exercise has suddenly taken on the enormous importance of a symbolic act. The speaker
explains that he longs to return to the branches of
his childhood when he's "weary of considerations,/ And life is too much like a pathless wood."
It is then that he would like "to get away from

101

earth awhile/ And then come back to it and begin over." And what better way to do this than to "swing on birches," that is, to come away alone, to climb above the furor of the crowd to let heart, soul, and mind come together in splendid unity.

So the last sentence of the poem is no longer a riddle. Now we can understand the poet's enthusiasm for birch-swinging—it represents the proper kind of self-reliance, the right sort of personal indulgence, the appropriate emphasis on one's individuality. And for each of God's sons and daughters, to swing on God's birches is to be involved in God's creation as He intended. And certainly "one could do worse than" that!

Robert Frost's "The Death of the Hired Man" is a dialog between a farmer and his wife about an old man, now no longer useful as a hired hand. The old man has returned to his former employer in the desperate hope to have one more season's work, one last summer's dignity for his fast-ebbing life.

We never see the old man (we are told he is asleep on a couch inside the parlor), but we do overhear a conversation between the farmer and his wife. They argue about the wisdom of bothering with the old man now that he can no longer be of much help. The wife recognizes that the old man is ill, and she also is sensitive enough to know that his talk about ditching the meadow and clearing the upper pasture was an attempt to save his self-respect.

The farmer, however, at first wants nothing to do with someone from whom a day's work is no longer possible. But when his wife points out that Silas, the hired man, has simply come home, the farmer admits, indeed, home is "the place where, when you have to go there,/ They have to take you in."

Warren, the farmer, slowly is led to a more sensitive position by the gentle prodding of his wife. Finally, after some extended conversation, he is prepared to welcome Silas back to help however the old man thinks he can. And then comes Frost's close:

103

Warren returned—too soon, it seemed to her,
Slipped to her side, caught up her hand and waited.
"Warren?" she questioned.
"Dead," was all he answered.

The reader who was pleased with the prospect
of reconciliation between Warren and Silas is dis-
appointed, but a major change has taken place in
the stubborn farmer—and the pitiful Silas has
been the catalyst for this change. He who had
nothing to offer threw himself on the mercy of the
only people he could go to, and they nearly rejected him. By making himself vulnerable to rejection, Silas forced Warren to make a decision. Making this decision in the final lines of the poem
enriches Warren's spirit and gives the poem its
heart.

Dylan Thomas, the beautifully lyrical Welsh poet, has left us some strong words about living—and about dying. Among his great legacy of poems is one he wrote for his father in the latter days of the man's life. After the first line, the poem, "Do Not Go Gentle into that Good Night," speaks of the need for struggle, for determination, for the avoidance of submission.

The poet says that neither "good men" nor "wise men" nor "wild men" nor "grave men" have learned how to "go gentle." Such men have been sustained by their contributions, by their love for life, by the vitality of what the future could hold. They have not been content to steal away into the shadows timidly and without murmur.

Besides encouragement to engage in some struggle with the inevitable, the poet begs his father to give him the model he needs for his own life and death, some final attitude by which his son can remember him.

And yet we know that the "good night" of which the poet speaks need hold no fears nor unexpected surprises. But nevertheless we want to hang onto life, no matter how unpleasant, because we are not sure of what is coming; most of us would choose known pain before some vague promise of bliss. Indeed, let us recognize that God gave us life to enjoy and we are careless stewards to let it go prematurely. However, when the time has come for it to end we are equally unwise to prolong what has been intended as just a short wait in the vestibule of eternity.

54

The widespread poverty of the thirties has become a part of American folklore, and many of those who suffered through those days speak readily about how difficult their lives were. Nowhere is this bone-throbbing destitution more clearly described than in John Steinbeck's monumental novel, *The Grapes of Wrath*. Its title is taken from a phrase in "The Battle Hymn of the Republic" where the Lord is described as "trampling out the vintage where the grapes of wrath are stored."

This 1939 novel tells the story of the Joad family. Blown from their sharecropping land by Oklahoma sand winds, the Joads believe California is the land of promise. So off they go—three generations of poor farmers, with a member of the fourth generation born along the way. They meet others as they travel down hot and unfriendly highways toward "paradise" in California; gas station attendants are surly, waitresses are friendly but cautious, and merchants are downright hostile. Still the Joads persevere and bring their rough sort of virtue and light to a host of needy people. They encourage the despairing one-eyed man to cover up his eye and get his life together, and a waitress sells bread and candy more cheaply after she tastes the milk of human sympathy.

The Grapes of Wrath is not a pretty story, but it is a moving and extremely gripping one. California was, of course, not the paradise the Joads sought.

The book does not end happily, with their discovering oil or benefitting from the favors of a rich land-owner. Rather, Steinbeck sums up the spirit of the book and the times with a tragic and poignant scene. The Joads, now reduced to living in boxcars, meet a young boy and his starving father in the pouring rain. The book's more than six hundred pages end with the young mother, Rose of Sharon, giving the starving man the milk intended for her baby, who has just died.

As a social document and description of human life, Steinbeck's novel has no peer in American fiction. It makes that difficult era shine clearly and honestly, and helps us remember and understand what it meant to drink the juice so painfully squeezed from the "grapes of wrath."

Thomas Stearns Eliot was one of this century's most articulate poets; he was also literary spokesman and defender of the Christian view of things. Several of his poems probe the bankrupt life of the new age and the "wasteland" in which modern man is content to dwell. Eliot creates a cast of characters he feels are typical of the puzzled denizens of this lost planet. Among these is J. Alfred Prufrock, a socially awkward man afraid to grow old.

In the poem "The Love Song of J. Alfred Prufrock," Eliot uses the "stream of consciousness" mode; that is, the speaker, Prufrock, expresses in an apparently random way what is flowing through his mind. He wants to declare his love for a certain woman. But he is so seized with feelings of inadequacy, he is so divided against himself, that he is finding it difficult even to get started.

At the poem's outset, in one of the more familiar passages in modern poetry, Prufrock tries to bring his divided self (the "you and I") together long enough to accomplish what he wants so desperately: "Let us go then, you and I,/ When the evening is spread out against the sky/ Like a patient etherized upon a table;/ Let us go, through certain half-deserted streets,/ The muttering retreats/ Of restless nights in one-night cheap hotels/ And sawdust restaurants with oyster shells:/ Streets that follow like a tedious argument/ Of insidious intent/ To lead you to an overwhelming question . . ./ Oh, do not ask, "What is it?"/ Let us go and make our visit."

With this rather balky beginning, Prufrock takes himself off to the room where "the women come and go/ Talking of Michelangelo," an intimidating state of affairs. He knows that he will have time for "a hundred indecisions,/ And for a hundred visions and revisions,/ Before the taking of a toast and tea."

As Prufrock makes his way toward his rendez-vous, he thinks of other impediments to his success: "And indeed there will be time/ To wonder, 'Do I dare?' and, 'Do I dare?'/ Time to turn back and descend the stair,/ With a bald spot in the middle of my hair—/ (They will say: 'How his hair is growing thin?')" And on it goes.

The neurotic and besetting fears of Prufrock are the fears of modern man, says Eliot. Prufrock puts much of this in a clearer light when he admits that he has measured out his life with coffee spoons. He also confesses that the eyes of strangers some-times make him feel like an insect "pinned and wriggling on the wall."

Is this the creature that God on the sixth day looked at and said was "good"? Is this he who has been made "a little lower than the angels" and has been "crowned with a crown of glory"? Hardly. In "The Love Song of J. Alfred Prufrock," an obtuse and often difficult poem, the poet Eliot has re-vealed the convictions of the Christian Eliot. Modern man has come to the point of social steril-ity, says Eliot—his experiment of trying to do without the guidance of his Creator has backfired. This has resulted in a race of men for whom even the merest experience of loving, the most casual

110

kind of caring, is filled with hesitation. The modern age has eclipsed that Source of light from which man must draw his strength and to which he must look for an Example of how to share himself—in portions considerably larger than coffee spoons.

56

H_e was born in St. Louis, but T. S. Eliot soon became an international traveler and scholar. He studied first at Harvard and then sailed for Paris to study the works of the French philosopher Henri Bergson. After crossing the Atlantic several more times, Eliot decided his literary future lay in England.

In many of his poetic images, Eliot captures the arid and sterile characters created by technology and the modern erosion of spiritual values. Time and again he describes unstable and flimsy people, buffeted about by the mildest breeze. This is literally true of "the hollow men," speakers in a poem of that title. Eliot seems especially bitter toward such people who accomplish nothing, either for good or for evil.

Eliot employs several techniques in "The Hollow Men" to communicate his message. There is a double epigraph: a line from Conrad's *Heart of Darkness* and a line spoken by English boys trying to collect money around Guy Fawkes Day. Then there is the parody of the children's rhyme, "Here we go round the mulberry bush," the use of partial lines from the Lord's Prayer, and several obscure literary allusions. This is, admittedly, complex; Eliot's poetry is wonderful, but it is seldom easy. His technique is often visual and impressionistic; those who would share the poet's vision of a flawed and mildewed world will have to read his work slowly and patiently.

Eliot's vision is essentially a Christian one, but he knows that it is not a matter of black and white hats, the "good" guys and the "bad." The world is inhabited by men who, although perhaps hollow spiritually, are sometimes capable of great achievements. It is one of civilization's great ironies that these men are impotent in the things which truly matter. In Eliot's poem, "the hollow men" end their declaration of who they are with the expressed fear that "This is the way the world ends/ Not with a bang but a whimper." This line, a subtle parody of the *Gloria Patri* ("As it was in the beginning, is now, and ever shall be, world without end. Amen"), indicates the tragic inability of modern man to sustain the promise of the world which has always been God's intention.

57

In 1935, with the shadow of war lengthening across the continent of Europe, T. S. Eliot wrote a powerful religious drama on the theme of fascism and Christian doctrine. Written at the behest of Canterbury Cathedral, *Murder in the Cathedral* is the story of Thomas à Becket, the twelfth-century archbishop whose ideas of proper rule and church business conflicted with those of the king. This clash caused Becket's exile, and eventually his death. Eliot makes Becket a proud and brilliant man whose suffering is a combination of his dissent with the king and his struggles with himself.

This inner conflict is skillfully illustrated by Eliot as Becket confronts each of four tempters who offer him a way out of his almost certainly fatal impasse with the king. The first temptation, easily spurned, is that Thomas lead an "easy," uncontroversial life with no trouble and no confrontation with the king. The second, as quickly dispatched as the first, is an appeal for power, a commodity which Becket has had and has tired of. The third temptation is a bit more subtle; it is to oppose the king, to set up a polemic not necessarily on any lofty issue, but just for the sake of balance and opposition. This idea appeals a bit more to Thomas, but he rejects it soon enough.

And then comes the fourth temptation, an encouragement that Becket die as a martyr. He could take full advantage of the church versus state issues, and wrap himself as tightly as possible in his

114

own robes of righteousness. He could die for the glory which would come to him after death. Becket admits that he has thought of this, and wrestles with his great burden of pride.

When his assassins finally come, Becket is ready to die—but not for the same reasons as before. He does not die as a proud martyr who manipulated his own reputation, but in defense of that church which Christ chose as His bride and against which not even the gates of hell will prevail.

And so it is for us to decide whether or not our sacrifices, modest though they be—our tithes, our time, our service, even our prayers—are made from a sense of love and loyalty or from a hope of reward.

Perhaps T. S. Eliot's most famous critical essay is "Tradition and the Individual Talent," in which he draws some striking analogies between the life-work of the artist and that of the Christian. Eliot says that the artist must not ignore all that has been written and experienced in the past. Rather, he ought to graft himself to it; he ought to add his contribution to the stream of tradition instead of trying to stem the flood with needless remoteness or obscurity.

Notice how Eliot's description of the artistic process echoes descriptions of the Christian's obligation:

> What happens is a continual surrender of himself as he is at the moment to something which is more valuable. The progress of an artist is a continual self-sacrifice, a continual extinction of personality.

Here we have a marvelous truth. It is necessary for each of us to submit to a greater power, a stronger call, a "more excellent way." This process of depersonalization is not, as many would insist, debilitating and incarcerating. Indeed, the current emphasis on "doing your own thing" will work neither for the artist nor for the Christian. Accomplishment can come only by surrender; true liberation comes by submission. If only the world could grasp the divine riddle, the paradox of the gospel: "He that loseth his life . . . shall find it."

T.S. Eliot's greatest poetic contribution came in the form of four complex poems, published together in 1943 under the title, *Four Quartets*. Each poem's title is a place name associated with Eliot's life; as a collection the poems reflect the complexities of contemporary civilization and the confusion that has resulted from the rejection of Christian truth.

Each poem has its own season and its own element. "Little Gidding," the last of the four, is devoted to winter and fire. It was written during World War II, and was named for an Anglican religious community north of London which had a positive influence in the dark days of the seventeenth-century Civil War in England. The fire in the poem represents both the pentecostal fire of the Holy Spirit and the fires burning in war-torn London; Eliot saw, as Coleridge said is true of all poets, "similarities in dissimilarities."

Coming to Little Gidding, says Eliot, gives one a deep feeling of the triviality of most of man's activities:

> You are not here to verify,
> Instruct yourself, or inform curiosity
> Or carry report. You are here to kneel
> Where prayer has been valid. And prayer is more
> Than an order of words, the conscious occupation
> Of the praying mind, or the sound of the voice praying.

Nor is the experience of the blitz and its damage entirely without merit. Nothing good comes without suffering; the fire of the German bombs and the fire of the Holy Spirit can both bring redemption and release. This is the paradox of the Christian faith and of Eliot's poetry:

> Who then devised the torment? Love.
> Love is the unfamiliar Name
> Behind the hands that wove
> The intolerable shirt of flame
> Which human power cannot remove.
> We only live, only suspire
> Consumed by either fire or fire.

60

Ash Wednesday, the first day of Lent, has long
been an important day on the Christian calendar.
T. S. Eliot's highly allusive poem, "Ash Wednesday," is concerned with the deep meanings of this
important occasion and uses complex imagery to
communicate spiritual truths.

One of these verities is the need for man to escape from the normal restraints of space and time.
Lent is traditionally a period of self-denial, and
the speaker in the poem is caught in that familiar
human conflict between sacrifice and indulgence,
between the spiritual and the temporal, between
the divine and the human urges. He says:

Because I know that time is always time
And place is always and only place
And what is actual is actual only for one time
And only for one place
I rejoice that things are as they are and
I renounce the blessed face
And renounce the voice
Because I cannot hope to turn again
Consequently I rejoice, having to construct something
Upon which to rejoice. . . .

Remembering that poetry, especially that written in the twentieth century, is often mental and
emotional shorthand, it is possible to see in these
lines the hope to know a "more excellent way," as
the Scriptures say. We are so often in contact with
the corruption and materialism of our culture that
we are tempted with the easy and the comfortable.

But "Ash Wednesday," both as Christian event and as poem, is a denial of this contentment and stands as a reminder of the purpose of our brief sojourn "in this brief transit where the dreams cross/ the dream-crossed twilight between birth and dying."

61

In his short poem, "Journey of the Magi," T. S. Eliot has one of the Christmas story's famous wise men describe that celebrated but little-known trip. He begins by saying that it was a "cold coming," made worse by the uncooperative camels, the unreliable helpers, and the unfriendly towns—to say nothing of mysterious voices which sounded in the travelers' ears "saying that this was all folly."

The second of the poem's three irregular stanzas speaks of a sudden change in all the unpleasantness. This occurred one dawn when the weary travelers came down out of the desert to "a temperate valley,/ Wet, below the snow line, smelling of vegetation." Even a first-time reader of Eliot's poetry should be aware that Eliot uses moisture and aridity as spiritual symbols: the more water, the more vegetation; the more vegetation, the more spiritual growth. The coming of the "temperate valley" is a clear indication that great spiritual values are at hand.

In stanza three, the speaker comes back to the present and asks a question which has obviously been occupying his mind in the years since his return. He wants to know, "Were we led all that way for/ Birth or Death?" Obviously this thoughtful magi had witnessed both, but until his journey he had thought they were distinguishable. Now he is not sure. As he says of the coming of the Child whom they celebrated: "This birth was/ Hard and bitter agony for us, like Death, our death." He is a man who has witnessed a life change, whose outlook will never again be the same. He is not quite sure what happened to him as a result of the confrontation with the remarkable Babe, but as he closes he admits that he "should be glad of another death."

The life/death paradox expressed by Eliot's magi is oft-discussed in the Gospels. John speaks of finding our life by losing it; while that seems a contradiction to the casual observer, it will be perfectly understood by anyone who has traveled the route of which the magi speaks. The believer, like the speaker in Eliot's poem, finds himself "no longer at ease with an alien people clutching their gods."

62

Of all the ingredients of worship, perhaps sound is among the most difficult to control, simply because there is so much of it. However, those responsible for the conduct of worship ought to be skilled in the use of sound and silence alike. Worshipers should, in turn, be sensitive to when sound and when silence is appropriate.

We use words to worship the Word when sometimes silence is far more suitable. Thomas Merton, the saintly and articulate Trappist monk, speaks of this when he says, "Corporate and liturgical prayer are indeed important in the life of the Church ... but they do not of themselves satisfy the deep need for intimate contact with God in solitary prayer." If we believe that God comes to us in personal revelation, that He deals with us one by one, then we ought even to devote part of our corporate worship time to an individual praising of God.

Many Christian worshipers have lost the sense of adoration which has so long been a part of the worship tradition. Since silence is so seldom a part of the world in which we live and work, we should deeply desire a time to be silent, especially in the presence of the Author of all things. The Quakers have long recognized this truth, and to them silence becomes a bridge, not of separation, but of communication.

Worship which is all silence goes too far, for humans need activity; but worship which has no silence can easily lose God in the shuffle of turning pages and muffled "amens."

63

Laura Wingfield is the heroine, if she may be called a heroine, of Tennessee Williams's *The Glass Menagerie*. She is a young woman in her early twenties, painfully shy, crippled, and under the control of a benevolent but tyrannical mother. Laura's days are largely taken up with caring for her collection of glass animals. The collection, which she keeps on several shelves, obviously represents the fragile and unreal world with which she has chosen to surround herself.

The play is concerned with the relationship Laura has with her restless brother; with her mother, who still remembers her days as the "belle of the ball"; and with a "gentleman caller," her brother's friend on whom Laura once had a secret crush.

Laura Wingfield's story echoes the situation of many people, young and old, who are kept from meaningful relationships by shyness or by feelings of personal inadequacy. These sad men and women live out their days in dark corners behind unfriendly barriers.

Laura's story ends optimistically, however. When Jim, the "gentleman caller," comes to dinner, Laura, predictably, feigns sickness and leaves the room. Later, however, when she and Jim are left alone, Laura shows him her glass collection and especially her dearest possession, a glass figure of a unicorn. The play's climax occurs when Jim accidentally knocks the unicorn off the shelf onto the floor, breaking its horn. With this the spell is broken. Laura offers Jim the broken animal, which now looks normal with its horn gone. We are led to believe that, like the hornless unicorn, Laura has taken a turn toward normality and, it would be hoped, to happiness.

Many people invest their time and emotions in their own "glass menageries" in order to avoid confronting the real world. By doing so, they avoid the natural progress which ought to be a part of the human experience. We grow by interaction, by mutual sharing, and even by disagreement and controversy. God did not plan for man to be isolated or estranged from his fellowmen. To be alone or unable to relate to others contradicts the divine scheme for human growth. Indeed, this growth will, as best we know, continue when we arrive in God's presence.

64

The keynote play of the postwar era may be *No Exit*. In it Jean-Paul Sartre, the father of the modern existentialist novel and drama, pits together three rather unsavory characters after death. Garcin is a Hemingway-type character who had always prided himself on being masculine, but who died by firing squad after trying to desert the army; Estelle is a woman of loose morals who was executed for killing her baby; and Inez, a lover of women, is cynical and tough.

The three meet in a room which we are told is "hell," and they each begin to play one against the other in sadistic bitterness. When Garcin tries to escape his two female tormentors, the only door in the room will not open at first. When, after much effort, it does open, Garcin finds himself powerless to go through it. For the room's three occupants there is "no escape." Garcin sums up their—and modern man's—dilemma when he defines hell. He explains that the old idea of hell as fire and brimstone is wrong. "Hell," he says in the last minute of the play, "is other people." Although it misses the mark of biblical revelation, Garcin's conclusion does sensitively express the feeling of modern man that there is "no exit" from the dilemma of living.

Try as he may, man cannot hope to rescue himself from this cul-de-sac of confusion. Sartre recognizes this plight. But with his atheistic brand of existentialism, he is powerless to offer a remedy.

The gospel message, on the other hand, will open up life to loving human community— rather than escape from people—through liberating fellowship with Him who made us. For indeed, God still holds the exclusive rights to our happiness.

Poetry does not always contain beautiful images or picturesque descriptions of pastoral scenes. Sometimes it is downright grotesque, with raw power giving insight into man's cruelty and self-ishness. Such a poem is "More Light! More Light!" by the contemporary poet, Anthony Hecht. Taking his title from the presumed last words of Goethe, the German poet and scientist, Hecht draws our attention to two episodes, separated in history by four centuries. The first is a description of the execution of Bishop Nicholas Ridley, burned at Oxford for heresy in 1553:

Nor was he forsaken of courage,
  but the death was horrible,
The sack of gunpowder failing to ignite.
His legs were blistered sticks on which the black sap
Bubbled and burst as he howled for the Kindly Light.

But, says the poet, this sort of inhumanity was not confined to a distant century or some esoteric religious controversy. In our own time we have known the depths of the human capacity for evil:

We move now to outside a German wood.
Three men are there commanded to dig a hole
In which the two Jews are ordered to lie down
And be buried alive by the third, who is a Pole.

No light, no light in the blue Polish eye.
When he finished, a riding boot packed down the earth.

The Luger hovered lightly in its glove.
He was shot in the belly and in three hours bled to
   death.

   The location of this actual incident is ironic,
and the poet is fully aware of the irony. Welmar,
near where this atrocity occurred, was the intellectual center of Germany during the eighteenth
and early nineteenth centuries. It is also near
Buchenwald, the Nazi death camp. Hecht recognized that no light was forthcoming from this area,
no matter how intellectual it was. Indeed the light
so surely lacking in both execution scenes cannot
be manufactured by man on his own. It comes
from God, who is constant Life and Light. He
loved us enough to save us from the horrible
cruelty we are all capable of when we are seduced
by a sense of self-importance. Man's pride blots
out the sun which gives us our indispensable
Light.

66

The hymnbook is at once the source of lovely and moving poetry and of doggerel which never should have seen the light of day. Among the former are those lovely pieces in *Olney Hymns*, published in 1782 by John Newton and William Cowper (pronounced "Cooper") at the height of the Wesleyan Revival; the book was named for the lovely English country town in which the two men lived. Many of the hymns are deeply personal and emotional, in the style of evangelical hymnody—none more so than Cowper's "There Is a Fountain Filled with Blood," inspired by the prophecy of Zechariah.

As is often the case in Cowper's poetry, the central figure of the hymn is "I," the poor, wandering soul who desperately seeks for salvation. "I" finds hope in the example of the "dying thief" in verse two, and in the vision of "the stream [Christ's] flowing wounds supply" in verse four. These experiences of the "I" are, says the poet, enough to keep him singing until this "poor lisping, stammering tongue lies silent in the grave"—a classic example of the self-depreciating lyrics often occurring in early evangelical hymnody.

William Cowper was a man whose life was threaded through with rare visions such as these, alternating with periods of deep depression and emotional instability. But this hymn, sung millions of times since its penning in that green corner of Buckinghamshire, shows that Cowper's concern for his soul was genuine and his quest for salvation, painful though it may have been, was not unsuccessful. Indeed, his songs have been helpful to many other seekers who have wanted to be "plunged beneath that flood."

67

There have been many periods of history when confusion reigned, when the people were troubled about the future, and when political and civil affairs seemed chaotic. One such period was in eighteenth-century England when Queen Anne, the last of the Stuart family, was dying. There was widespread anxiety about her successor and about the welfare of the British monarchy. To allay the people's fears the gifted hymnwriter, Isaac Watts, wrote his paraphrase of Psalm 90, entitled, "O God, Our Help in Ages Past."

What comforting words are these! God not only has been active on our behalf in the past; He is also "our hope for years to come." He has been active since "before the hills in order stood, or earth received her frame." Watts recognizes our vulnerability in "the stormy blast" of circumstance and calls upon God to be "our guard while life shall last" and then, recognizing even this is not enough, to be also "our eternal home."

No wonder this hymn is often used on national and special occasions; it was especially popular at the end of both world wars. The God of creation is also the God of history, and He has proved that His promise to stay with us until the end of time was given carefully and with concern for our constant vulnerability.

In the Middle Ages it was the wandering troubadour; during the Renaissance the court musician; for the Victorians the music hall singers; and for the modern era it is the rock singer who entertains us, with lyrics which reflect our fears and our loves, our highs and our lows, our victories and our defeats.

Suppose, in a hypothetical future century, an archaeologist picks through the rubbish of our civilization and comes upon a pile of gaily-colored square cardboard envelopes with round, thin plastic discs in them. If he discovers the message they contain, he will no doubt be convinced that the last half of the twentieth century was a sad time, a period filled with broken promises, jagged relationships, and a universal loneliness. If you are not sure of this, flick on your radio and listen to the less-than-encouraging words:

> I am, I said, and no one was there to hear, not even
> the chair. . . .
> Eleanor Rigby picked up the rice from the floor
> where the wedding had been. . . .
> Don't think, feel it's all right. . . .

These are already considered "classics" because they so solidly and fully represent the state of mind of many who live in the rush of modern life.

Contrast with these the words, "Rock of Ages, cleft for me," or, "A shelter in the time of storm," or, "We have an anchor that keeps the soul stead-

134

fast and sure while the billows roll." Note the difference between the tissue of temporary feeling to which modern man is often a victim and the granite of the eternal God. The pain and anguish described in much of modern music has no antidote; the hymns of Christ's church, on the other hand, bespeak that permanence and solidity which God has promised.

69

The idea of the Christian life as a battle against evil did not originate with Victorian hymnwriters infused with the spirit of the British Empire. Rather, it was begun, or at least greatly encouraged, by the apostle Paul in his letter to the Ephesian Christians. Paul instructed to "take unto you the whole armor of God, that ye may be able to withstand in the evil day"; further, they were to protect their loins with truth, their breasts (and hearts) with righteousness, and their feet with the "gospel of peace" (Eph. 6:13–15).

Among the many hymns which have taken up the Christian soldier theme is Charles Wesley's fine old piece, "Soldiers of Christ, Arise," which is based directly on the passage in Ephesians. At the beginning of this hymn we are called upon to stir ourselves, arise and "put [our] armor. But we are also given the promise that we will not have to rely on our own strength, but rather in that "which God supplies/ Through His eternal Son." Wesley then borrows from Romans 8 and tells us that he to whom the strength of Jesus is given is "more than conqueror."

Perhaps the greatest single point of Wesley's hymn is that we cannot possibly fight in our own strength; those who are seduced into taking the self-reliant route are doomed to failure. We are admonished to "stand then in His great might" and to arm ourselves with "the panoply of God" so that, when with all "conflicts past," we will

136

"o'ercome through Christ alone/ And stand complete at last."

Though written two hundred years ago, Wesley's words still speak to a society influenced by talk-show guests and paperback writers trumpeting the virtue of ME. Wesley's hymn is a wise counter to the forces that encourage us to try to make it on our own with no help, temporal or otherwise.

Even the most humanistic writers concede that the world is a constant battlefield. It is tragic that they cannot see that only God's armor is impenetrable.

70

Worship carries us away from the mundane and sublunary life we lead. One reason worship is successful in doing this is that time, as we ordinarily consider it, is not an ingredient of worship. There is a great timelessness about the creeds, for instance, or about the prayers, or even the great hymns. The attitude of quiet and waiting before God in worship is anticipatory of that future hour (note how time is inescapable even in our language) "when the trumpet of the Lord shall sound/ and time shall be no more."

Worship, then, is as close as we can come on earth to experiencing the Kingdom. When we come together to share in the praising of God— whether this takes place in cathedrals with stained glass or in a storefront with broken glass—we are part of a microcosm within which hours and minutes should have no meaning.

This is admittedly the ideal, and it has been achieved again and again by those who recognize they need respite from the pressing considerations of time. Worship creates a spiritual vacuum where the Holy Spirit can do His work, for the voice of God is not drowned out by the ticking of the clock.

The clergyman or other spiritual leader responsible for the conduct of worship has a further responsibility. He must prepare himself for the rarefied atmosphere which ought to accompany any worship experience, and must communicate to those who worship with him that attitude of reverence and regard for eternality. This is essential if the petty concerns of the working day, with its time clock and lunch whistle, are to be replaced by the presence of the One who said, "Before Abraham was, I AM."

71

What do poetry and worship have in common?
More than might appear at first glance. Both represent an elevation of the human spirit and vision
to a level considerably above that of the daily
routine. Every man has a deep-seated need for
poetry and worship, for both of these offer a refuge
from the crassness and insensitivity of a society
dedicated to material acquisition. Why, then, are
these sacred activities often given such little attention?

Churches are, ideally, places of meditation and
holy quiet. We can find noise anywhere, but worship is intended to be a release from the ordinary,
an avoidance of the mundane, an escape out of the
routine. But silence and meditation are so antithetical to the contemporary way of life that, unfortunately, modern man feels uncomfortable and
inept in such an environment.

Nor is poetry much more popular. We have lost
the desire to sit down with a volume of lyrics or an
epic and let our mind be stimulated with the
music of ordered language and the power of great
imagery. When we do pause to read, it is usually a
magazine or newspaper, or at best fast-moving
mystery. Not that these are bad, of course, but we
are a great deal poorer if we ignore the appeal of
poetry.

There is something ethereal and cleansing
about good poetry which cannot occur even in the
best fiction. Poetry is the concentrated and elliptic

record of common experience; part of its attraction is the beauty and power of its language.

In both poetry and worship, man can find surcease for his deepest needs. In poetry, he can find his own experience reflected in skillful language and precision of metaphor, and can feel one with others who also have suffered and rejoiced, stumbled and conquered. In worship, this same man can experience jubilation in his soul as he is lifted above his ordinary thoughts and, as in poetry, feels his common bond with fellow worshipers. The worshiper is also made aware of his unique nature in the sight of God, the One who made him, and who, in love, gave him poetry to enjoy.

72

Those who believe in God and who consider the Bible His message to mankind sometimes take lightly the Bible's literary dimensions. To say that the Bible uses metaphor or personification is not to demythologize it, water down its potency, or question its authenticity and effectiveness, as some fear. The biblical writers, while working under divine inspiration, used the devices and techniques of other good writers; these methods aid immeasurably in the communication of the Scripture's spiritual message.

This "literariness" can be illustrated by using the familiar example of Psalm 23. Here we have a metaphor at the very beginning: "The Lord is my shepherd." It is clear that this poem is being written from the "viewpoint" of a sheep, although obviously sheep cannot think logically or express themselves in written form. This means that the writer has assumed a "persona," and an effective one it is. The speaker/sheep is content to be led by the shepherd, for he knows that not only will he be brought into pleasant places but that he will be kept safe when danger comes.

Now and again the narrator expresses very unsheeplike ideas, as in, "He restoreth my soul." But that makes no difference, since we know it is not actually a sheep speaking, but rather a man who is describing his relationship to God in terms of a sheep's relationship with its shepherd. We know that sheep do not eat at "prepared tables" or have

142

"cups which run over," but the writer combines the sheep and human characteristics so well that the transition is made with no objection by the reader.

What does the use of these literary techniques mean to the reader in search of assurance or spiritual comfort? The answer to this is clear: Like many other literary methods used in the Bible, the object in Psalm 23 is to express the intensely personal and often complex relationship between man and God in simple terms which can be understood by nearly everyone. The poem successfully expresses a confidence and delight on the part of the sheep which, the reader infers, can be his as well if he will allow himself to be led by the Lord near waters, through valleys, and finally, to rest.

Even the most casual Bible reader recognizes that Scripture is full of wisdom and knowledge. This is particularly true of a certain Old Testament book which seems to be nothing *but* wisdom, written in the best possible form to communicate its wisdom to readers. This book was written by several persons, including the principal contributor, King Solomon of Israel—who represents the epitome of wisdom to the Judaeo-Christian world.

The Book of Proverbs, attributed to Solomon, is the best of ancient wisdom and concerns itself with many subjects: pride, temperance, the use of wealth, indolence, and the fear of God, to name only a few. By the time the reader finishes Proverbs, he cannot help but feel himself pinned against the wall and measured. Such statements as, "The fear of the Lord is the beginning of wisdom: and the knowledge of the holy is understanding" (9:10) are penetrating and searching indeed.

However, it is not only the content but the form which makes Proverbs effective. There is a syntactical balance, an attractive symmetry to the poetry which makes it memorable and easy to assimilate. The second phrase of a single poetic idea confirms and develops the first phrase. It is, to use a crude analogy, something like a seesaw, with weight evenly distributed on each side. Look at these examples to understand what I mean:

Trust in the Lord with all thine heart;
And lean not unto thine own understanding (3:5).

The labor of the righteous tendeth to life:
The fruit of the wicked to sin (10:16).

He that oppresseth the poor reproacheth his Maker:
But he that honoureth him hath mercy on the poor
(14:31).

So it is the form as well as the theme, the shell as well as the nut, that is important here. And therein lies an important literary principle: good literature seldom contains rare or exotic ideas (there are few left!), but a great deal of its value is in its mode of expressing those ideas, in its ability to give us "what oft was tho't, but ne'er so well expressed."

When we drink at the sweet well of Proverbs, we not only are pleased with the taste of God's water, but also with the shape of the gourd from which we sip.

In the Bible, when God chose to reveal the future to a particular man, He almost always used a dream or vision. When God wanted to show His glory to Isaiah, He did it with a vision of the six-winged seraphim (Isa. 6). When He wanted to show Amos what would happen to an unrepentant people, He showed him locusts, fire, the plumb line, a fruit basket, and the smitten sanctuary (Amos 7). When He wanted to illustrate for Ezekiel the nadir of spiritual death, He took him among the dry bones (Ezek. 37). These visions were real, and they were given for the same reason all metaphors are used: to give an earthly, concrete, comprehensible form to a divine mandate or prophetic mission.

The use of visions and dreams is common in literature of every tradition—from Egyptian hieroglyphics to Tevye's dream in the musical, *Fiddler on the Roof.* Of the scriptural visions, the most consistently intriguing is the complex vision of the apostle John on the Isle of Patmos, which is recorded in the final book of the New Testament. Like Daniel, its shorter, Old Testament companion, the Book of Revelation is essentially a chronicle of conflict. It describes the great, universal struggle between God, the Creator, and Satan, the pretender and would-be usurper. The Book of Revelation is, in fact, a series of fifteen connected (though not always clearly interpretable) visions. As with all biblical visions, these are full of warnings and exhortations, as well as a prophecy of the triumph of God and the suppression of the forces of evil.

Some Bible readers are uncomfortable with the visionary narratives which occur from time to time in the book, a discomfort which springs mainly from uncertainty about final interpretation and meaning. This is understandable, but we must remember that Scripture is for the direct benefit of the children of God; divine revelation is not meant to confuse or mislead. Indeed, it is not surprising that such an enormous spectacle as the conflict between evil incarnate and the Creator of all things cannot be described in ordinary or commonplace terms.

The visions recorded in the Bible, however difficult or complex, are an indispensable part of its intellectual-literary identity as well as of its spiritual purpose. By reading and trying to understand these visionary messages, we are seeing through the dark glass of our mortality a little more clearly, and it is even possible that we can catch a glimmer of the gem of truth.